MORE HOT

# MORE HOT TOPICS

## Bill Myers

# VICTOR BOOKS®

A DIVISION OF SCRIPTURE PRESS PUBLICATIONS INC.
USA  CANADA  ENGLAND

***More Hot Topics*** *gives the Bible's answers to questions that teenagers in youth groups are asking. It includes such topics as the New Age, evolution, heaven and hell, sex, and suffering. Student activity booklets (Rip-Off Sheets) and a leader's guide with visual aids (SonPower Multiuse Transparency Masters) are available from your local Christian bookstore or from the publisher.*

Scripture taken from the *Holy Bible, New International Version,* © 1973, 1978, 1984, International Bible Society. Used by permission of Zondervan Bible Publishers. Other Scripture quotations are from the *New American Standard Bible* (NASB), © the Lockman Foundation 1960, 1962, 1963, 1968, 1971, 1972, 1973, 1975, 1977, and from *The Living Bible* (TLB), © 1971, Tyndale House Publishers, Wheaton, IL 60189. Used by permission.

Cover illustration: Paul Turnbaugh

For information on booking Bill for lectures, retreats, or speaking engagements, please write Bill Myers in care of SonPower Youth Sources, 1825 College Avenue, Wheaton, IL 60187.

Library of Congress Catalog Card Number: 88-62914

ISBN: 0-89693-670-8

Recommended Dewey Decimal Classification: 248.83
Suggested Subject Heading: YOUTH—RELIGIOUS LIFE

© 1989, SP Publications, Inc. All rights reserved.
Printed in the United States of America.

# CONTENTS

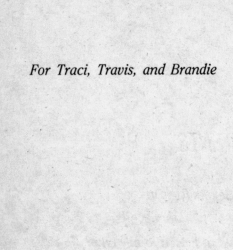

*For Traci, Travis, and Brandie*

# SEXUAL RIP-OFFS

▶ *Hey there, friends and neighbors—does your life have any semblance of fun? Do you occasionally find yourself actually having to put up with happiness, good times, or, worse yet, that feared and dreaded sensation of ... pleasure? Well, your suffering days are over. Just sign up for this here program called "Christianity" and I guarantee you your good times will come to an end. Why, God will give you so many do's and don'ts that you'll never have to endure another moment of joy again!*

Unfortunately, that's how lots of people view Christianity—as a bunch of rules and regulations.

Our motto: "If it's fun, it's sin."

But that's not at all what God has in mind. Jesus says He came here for the opposite reason.

> I came that you might have life and
> have it abundantly.
>
> John 10:10 (NASB)

That's what God wants. He wants us to experience life—abundant life—life at the absolute maximum . . . all its highs, all its beauties, all its wonders. He wants us to experience life so intensely that it is literally overflowing.

That's one of the reasons He's so down on sin—not because He doesn't want people to have good times, but because, in reality, sin steals those good times. In the long run it steals life—it rips us off of the very abundance He wants us to experience.

*Hold it a minute. Who are you kidding? Sin is fun.*

Absolutely. Anyone who won't admit that is probably already dead. But sin is also a trick—a baited hook. The first couple of bites will always taste great. But it isn't too long before we start feeling that hook, before it starts sinking in, before it starts robbing us of the very things it promised to deliver.

Keep that in mind as we begin looking for God's answers to these tough questions. Keep in mind that He's *always* on our side, that any guidelines He may have are for our own good. Keep in mind that He wants us to experience this life He created to its maximum capacity—thoroughly and "abundantly."

And nowhere is this more true than in the area of sex.

## ▶ *PRETTY GOOD STUFF*

Let's face it, as far as inventions go, God gets an A+ for this one. When properly enjoyed between two people, sex can be the most intimate, personal, and enjoyable form of communication in the world.

But when misused, it can shred hearts, scar souls, ruin the pleasure, and destroy the very relationship it was intended to build.

## ▶ *WHY WAIT?*

In the original *Hot Topics, Tough Questions,* we spent an entire chapter on this subject, explaining how outraged God is at premarital sex and discovering His severe warnings to those who continue to practice it: "Their place will be in the fiery lake of burning sulfur" (Rev. 21:8).

We also took a look at *why* God is so unyielding on the subject. First we examined some of the physical problems that modern-day sociologists are discovering to be *directly associated* with premarital sex. Problems like these:

> —The epidemic proportions of teen pregnancies. Today *one out of three* girls who have premarital sex is getting pregnant. One out of three!
> —The astronomical disease rate. Gonorrhea, syphilis, herpes II, AIDS—you name it, it's out there and spreading like wildfire *among young people.*

But these are only the physical problems. There are some others that run just as deep but are less visible. There is now clear scientific evidence that sex before marriage damages our emotions, our relationships (present and future), and our ability to actually enjoy sex to its fullest.

Some of this information has been compiled by Dr. Ray E. Short, a professor of sociology whose findings indicate:

—"Nonvirgins tend to have less happy marriages than virgins."

—"Nonvirgins are more apt to split up or be divorced after marriage than virgins."

—"Persons who have had premarital sex are more likely to cheat on their spouse (commit adultery) after they are married."

—"While those with previous sex experience say they do *adjust quicker* in their sex life after the wedding . . . the virgins are *more happy with their total sex life* in marriages than the nonvirgins."

—"Nonvirgins often get trapped into poor marriages by 'flunking the test of time.' Their good sex life fools them into thinking they have a good total adjustment when they do not. They marry and soon wish they had not."

—"The guilt, fear, and low self-regard that is felt in premarital sex will carry over and help spoil the sex life of the pair after marriage."

(From *Sex, Dating and Love,* Augs-
burg, pp. 71–72)

These are just a few of the reasons God's so
upset with premarital sex. If you're interested in
more detailed information, pick up a copy of the
original *Hot Topics, Tough Questions.* But for
now we have to move on; there are just too many
other areas we should discuss, too many other
areas where the enemy is ripping us off about sex.

## ▶ HEAVY MAKING OUT

Now before you figure you're reading some 18th-
century prude and decide to shred this book for
kitty litter, hear me out.

As we've already discussed, God's not too keen
on the sin of premarital sex. But He's also not too
thrilled about getting someone so worked up that
they *want* to sin:

> Things that cause people to sin are
> bound to come, but woe to that person
> through whom they come. It would be
> better for him to be thrown into the
> sea with a millstone tied around his
> neck than for him to cause one of
> these little ones to sin. So watch
> yourselves.
>
> Luke 17:1-3

Tough words. It's a safe guess that God's not
only bummed by sex before marriage but also by
heavy, getting-it-on times.
*Why?*

Well, first of all, there's always that chance of going over the line—of having to endure all the emotional, spiritual, and physical garbage that comes with premarital sex.

But even if that doesn't happen, there are still other reasons to avoid steaming up the old car windows—especially with someone you love. We've discussed it before (in *Hot Topics, Tough Questions,* pp. 43–44), but it's important enough to mention again.

> . . . Such situations rip off you and your partner. They get a fire started that as Christians you're forbidden to put out. So you sit there smoldering, frustrated, with only one thing on your mind. What type of atmosphere is that to build a relationship in? How do you get to know what someone is *really* like? How do you share spiritually? How do you do any of this when all you're thinking about is what you can't have?
>
> *But exactly how far can I go?*
>
> Sorry, no answer. That's between you two and the Holy Spirit. A good rule of thumb is to stop whenever your sexual feelings are being aroused to the point that they're trying to take over. But as to the exact moment, I can't help. If you feel guilty doing what you're doing, then stop. That's the Holy Spirit's conviction. I know this

sounds radical, but discuss the situation with your date. If you're seeing each other more and more, it might be a good idea to set up some parameters. Talk and pray about what you feel God would have you do and not do.

Praying about and discussing the situation doesn't have to be embarrassing. In fact, *it can draw a couple much closer together*. After all, what could be more personal than discussing your beliefs about Jesus and sex? Not only do you respect each other more, but your communication channels are deepened as you relate on a more personal and intimate level.

So, while the rest of the world is getting it on, going through all the wrestling holds but never really touching each other's hearts, the Christian couple can be getting to know one another much more deeply and intimately.

*And if we're already over our heads?*

Talk about it. Decide how to change your dating habits, how to avoid those tempting situations. Pass on those secluded parking spots, find a replacement for those make-out times in front of the TV. Go for something different. Spend more times with groups. Be creative; use your imagination. Try different activities like tennis, skating, skiing, swimming, biking, picnics, amusement parks, the zoo, ball games, museums, photography, hobbies, youth groups—the list goes on.

The point is, if you . . .

- are serious about pleasing God,
- want to develop a deeper relationship with your boyfriend or girlfriend,
- or just don't want to rip yourselves off, then find ways that still allow you to grow closer without focusing so much on the physical. In the long run you'll be much happier—and so will God.

## ▶ PORNOGRAPHY

Lately it seems more and more difficult to find the line where pornography begins. It used to be with *Playboy* or *Hustler*. But now it's tough to turn on the old tube without seeing the obligatory roll in the hay. Or to flip through some women's magazines without finding a couple of perfect bods clutched in a passionate embrace. Then of course there are movies. . . .

So, once again, I can't give a clear-cut answer on where porno begins . . . but if you find yourself gawking at something to get all worked up—congratulations, you've found it.

Before we get too deep into this subject, let's see what Jesus has to say. Keep in mind there weren't a lot of videos or foldouts around at the time. But His words about dwelling and drooling on sexy sights are just as valid today as back then:

I tell you that anyone who looks at a

woman lustfully has already committed adultery with her in his heart. If your right eye causes you to sin, gouge it out and throw it away. It is better for you to lose one part of your body than for your whole body to be thrown in hell.

Matthew 5:28-29

Sure sounds like He means business. But why? Why is it so important to God? Why is it so wrong to "look lustfully" at photos, videos, or the real thing?

## PORNOGRAPHY DESTROYS THE PERSON.

It tempts and taunts with something it can't deliver. At worst, it creates so much sexual tension that the viewer's standards are eaten away, making him more susceptible to sin. At best, it leaves the viewer smoldering in frustrations that he can do nothing about (except be ticked at God for not letting him do something).

It's addictive. Like any drug, you need more and more the get the same thrill. And with that desire to get more, the user finds somewhere down the line that he can't get by without it.

It feeds the old nature. If you've become a Christian, your spirit has been "reborn"; you're free from the old and can have a new, Christlike nature—if you want. But if you keep feeding the old nature with sin and lust, it starts to come back. It gains more and more control until it's once again calling the shots and controlling you.

## PORNOGRAPHY DESTROYS PLEASURE
It warps your thinking. Nobody in the world
looks (or performs) as good as those actors and
actresses—not even the actors and actresses
themselves (that's why so much money's spent on
lighting, directing, makeup, and air brushing).
Yet this fantasy world becomes the standard by
which the viewer judges his reality. And since
reality is *never* as good as fantasy, the viewer will
never be fully satisfied with real sex. He will
always feel ripped off.

It deprives enjoyment. Instead of experiencing
the deepest, most personal communication between two people, the person whose head is full
of porn is so busy going for the gymnastics and
superficial pleasures that the real depth and experience of sex completely elude him.

## PORNOGRAPHY DESTROYS RELATIONSHIPS
It distorts your view of people. You begin looking
at members of the opposite sex as pleasure toys
or as something to use—instead of as human beings to love and care for.

Pornography warps the ability to express love
to your partner. Instead of being the most intimate time of loving and giving, sex becomes a
wrestling match of taking and performing.

Tim LaHaye, a pastor, author, and family
counselor puts it best in *The Battle for the Family* (p. 179):

> I would judge that fully two-thirds of
> the sexual problems in marriage today

can be traced to the use of pornography.

On the surface, sex before marriage, heavy making out, and pornography may seem like minor indulgences. Maybe if people are enjoying it and nobody's getting hurt, then it shouldn't be that big a deal.

But the point is *EVERYBODY'S* getting hurt. Anybody involved in these practices is not only hurting himself but is hurting and ripping off those he comes in contact with.

It may be true that at first glance God seems like a killjoy for forbidding these things—for "depriving us" of them. But—as with all sin—when we look carefully, we see the hook. We see He's not depriving; He's protecting. He's not wanting to withhold; He's wanting to bless . . . *ABUNDANTLY.*

# SEXUAL COUNTERFEITS

▶ *SOLO SEX*

This is a tough subject to discuss. To be honest, masturbation (touching or rubbing your own sex organs for pleasure) isn't mentioned much in the Bible. And yet for millions of Christian teens (and adults) there are few issues that cause so much guilt, shame, and self-disgust.

These committed Christians have prayed, they've cried, they've tried again and again to stop, and still they haven't found freedom. The pleasure or emotional release that masturbation provides consumes and overshadows any earnest desire they have to do what they feel the Lord wants.

*So is it wrong?*
Probably.
Here's why:

ONE—When people masturbate, they almost always wind up fantasizing about someone—and as we've seen in Matthew 5:28-29, God's not real happy about that.

Also, as we talked about in our discussion of pornography, no human being in the world can make love to compare with our fantasies. So, when a person who masturbates finally does get married, there's a good chance he or she may be disappointed with a real sex life.

TWO—According to Romans 1:18-29, if something feels like a sin to you but you keep on doing it, you're probably going against God's "inner voice." In short, if something feels like sin and you keep on doing it, it *is* sin.

THREE—You're giving into the lust battle inside your head and ignoring the command to "abstain from sinful desires, which war against your soul" (1 Peter 2:11).

It's true, everyone of us has that civil war going on inside our minds. But the more times you win, the more times you "abstain," the stronger you'll become and the more control you'll have.

FOUR—And finally, you may be ripping yourself off in the enjoyment department. As you wind up programming the sex part of your thinking to just go for the physical pleasures, it may be very difficult later for you to enjoy the emotional side of sex—that deeper sharing and communication with your lifelong partner.

## ▶ SOMETHING WORSE

Even though there's a good chance that masturbation is wrong, there's something that is much worse: *THE GUILT AND SELF-HATRED THAT FOLLOW.*

I can't tell you the number of sincere Christians I've run into that think they're God's biggest disappointment because they can't seem to stop.

*Of course I know God forgives—but for how long? Until I stop, I'll never be anything to Him but a second-rate child.*

Guess again.

If you're *seriously* trying to stop and if you're going to Jesus and asking for forgiveness each time you fail, then *relax*. He understands. He's on your side.

If you are seriously sorry, and if you are really trying to quit, there's no sin that Jesus will not forgive over and over and over—and over some more.

Because . . .

> If we confess our sins, He is faithful and just and will forgive us our sins and purify us from all unrighteousness.
>
> 1 John 1:9

That doesn't mean we shouldn't keep fighting the fight and striving for victory. What it does mean is that if God loves and forgives us, we ought to be able to do the same.

Give yourself a break. God has.

## ▶ SOME POINTERS

If you're caught up in solo sex and feel the Lord wants you to get free of it, here are some helpful tips.

1. The lust battle is won or lost in the brain. And the brain is something you can control. So watch what you let it think. Don't let it dwell on steamy pictures or movies. Don't let it drift into sexy fantasies. Instead, force it to think about something else. You can control your thinking; it doesn't have to control you.

2. Keep going to Jesus for forgiveness and help. You may keep stumbling for a period of time, but when you fall make sure you're falling into His open arms. He'll *always* be there to catch you, forgive you, and lift you back up.

3. Don't hate yourself when you fail. God doesn't—and *never* will. That condemning voice you hear (after you've asked for forgiveness) is not from God. That's the devil trying to make you feel like garbage. That's "the accuser of our brothers, who accuses them [us] . . . day and night" (Revelation 12:10).

Satan's a liar. Don't fall for the creep's tactics. In fact, turn the tables on him.

4. Start using your times of failure as times to thank and worship the Lord for His endless love and forgiveness. Because if you're serious and trying, *IT MAKES NO DIFFERENCE HOW MANY TIMES YOU FAIL.* God will still love you and forgive you.

For I am convinced that neither death

> nor life, neither angels nor demons,
> neither the present nor the future, nor
> any powers, neither height nor depth,
> nor anything else in all creation, will
> be able to separate us from the love of
> God that is in Christ Jesus our Lord.
>
> Romans 8:38-39

If you're serious and trying, no amount of failure will separate you from the mercy and love of God.

And, in the end, you *WILL* win. Because . . .

> We are more than conquerors through
> Him who loved us.
>
> Romans 8:37

## ▶ HOMOSEXUALITY

Gay. What a cruel word. If ever there's a person who isn't happy and gay in today's world, it's the homosexual. Not only do gays face prejudice, misunderstanding, and hatred by the straight world (Christians included), they are faced with one of the cruelest rip-offs and counterfeits of sexuality there is.

As we begin, let's take a look at one of several references the Bible has on the subject:

> God gave them over to shameful lusts.
> Even their women exchanged natural
> relations for unnatural ones. In the
> same way the men also abandoned nat-
> ural relations with women and were
> inflamed with lust for one another.

> Men committed indecent acts with
> other men, and received in themselves
> the due penalty for their perversion.
> Romans 1:26-27

Homosexual activity is a sin. Make no mistake
about it. But God's response to it is no different
than to adultery, or sex before marriage, or any
number of other sins. Hard to believe? Then see if
you can find any distinctions made among those
who commit these different sins:

> Do not be deceived: Neither the sexual-
> ly immoral nor idolators nor adulterers
> nor male prostitutes nor homosexual
> offenders nor thieves nor the greedy
> nor drunkards nor slanderers nor
> swindlers will inherit the kingdom of
> God.
> 1 Corinthians 6:9-10

So those who smugly think homosexuality is
some terrible sin worse than greed, or spreading
untrue rumors, or being a drunk had better think
again. God's response is the same as it is to all
sin. No more—no less. He hates it. He hates it
because, like all sin, it:
- DISOBEYS His commands;
- DESTROYS His people;
- DEPRIVES them of His fullest blessing;
- DISTORTS what He created for good.

But God desperately wants to help those that
want His help—those who admit they're sinning
and want to stop. God hates the sin, but He loves

the sinner who wants to repent.

## ▶ HOW IT BEGINS

Although there are extremely rare exceptions, almost no one is born a homosexual. Let me repeat that. Except in the rarest of cases *NO ONE* is born a homosexual. Here is what Desert Stream Ministries (a Los Angeles-based organization designed to help the homosexual) has learned:

> Although research teams have spent much time and money trying to prove that homosexuality is inborn, no concrete proof has been found. In fact, famous researchers like Masters and Johnson state in their book *Human Sexuality,* "The genetic theory of homosexuality has been generally discarded today." Masters and Johnson also state that "despite the interest in possible hormone mechanisms in the origin of homosexuality, no serious scientist today suggests that a simple cause-effect relationship applies." (Desert Stream Ministries, "Understanding Homosexuality")

Homosexuality is not genetic. And it is not based on hormone imbalance. No one is born a homosexual. Most studies indicate that homosexuality is learned.

There are over 900 variables that can lead a person into homosexuality. And almost all of them involve extreme hurt, rejection, and a desperate need for affection. Let's discuss a typical scenario.

An extremely young child—let's say a boy—is hurt, rejected, or ignored by the parent of his sex—his father. To avoid this hurt, that boy withdraws even further from his dad or focuses on his mom—how she gets attention and affection, how she gets love.

As the boy matures, he begins to look to the same sex for the love and attention he so desperately needed from his father. Finally, as an adolescent, he begins to misinterpret and translate emotional needs into sexual ones. The need for love and affection from the same-sex parent is transferred to physical needs.

No one wakes up overnight and says, "Oh boy, I think I'll become a homosexual." It's a long, sad, painful process of rejection and a cry for love—a cry that breaks God's heart.

But what's sadder still is that many feel they are doomed to live this way forever.

*I was born this way; this is how I am naturally; there's nothing I can do about it.*

Wrong.

Homosexuality is a learned behavior. And the good news is that, like any learned behavior, it can be unlearned. It may not be easy and it may not happen overnight. But if the person really wants to fulfill that deep hunger for love, really wants to experience the fullest joy of sex, really wants to be all that God had originally intended, there is definitely a way to be free. Remember, it was Jesus Himself who said:

He has sent me to proclaim freedom
for the prisoners.

Luke 4:18

And . . .

If the Son sets you free, you will be
free indeed.

John 8:36

## ▶ HOW?

It would be tough to adequately cover the steps in
these few pages. But if you're one of the 5 to 10
percent of Americans struggling with homosexual
feelings, or if you know someone who is, here are
a few pointers to start out with.

### STEP ONE: BELIEVE

Believe that you can be free. Believe that Jesus is
telling the truth when He says He can heal you.
Don't believe you were born this way and are now
some hopeless victim. Hopelessness is the world's
thinking, not God's. It's my experience that God
works best in "impossible" situations.

### STEP TWO: PRAY

Nothing is impossible with prayer. Nothing.

I tell you the truth, My Father will give
you whatever you ask in My name. Until now you have not asked for anything in My name. Ask and you will
receive, and your joy will be complete.

John 16:23-24

## STEP THREE: SEEK COUNSEL

Find a mature believer in Christ who really understands the love of God (no bigots, please, and *not* someone you think has the same problem.)

Once you find the right person or persons, open yourself up to them. It'll be scary, but you have to expose those darkest, most fearful areas of your life. Because *darkness will flee only as it's exposed to light.*

Begin to pray, study, and talk with this person. You need not, you *cannot* fight this battle on your own. You need someone to help you experience how God can:

- replace your loneliness with His presence;
- heal your emotional hurts and remove your fear with His love;
- forgive all sin and completely break its hold over you.

## STEP FOUR: UNDERSTAND YOURSELF

Stop hating yourself. Keep reminding yourself that God loves you and counts you one of His *MOST PRIZED* possessions. Understand that your sexual feelings and needs are OK to have—they're just misdirected.

## STEP FIVE: REPROGRAM YOUR THINKING

I'm not talking about running out and getting married or throwing yourself in bed with the opposite sex. But, on a day-to-day basis, keep reminding yourself that you are the sex you are and that you were created in God's image. When those other thoughts come, when the homosexual thinking tries to take over, just gently push it out of your head and replace it with the truth. Instead of going by your feelings, choose to believe God's promises.

## STEP SIX: EXODUS INTERNATIONAL

There is an international ministry that fully understands the struggles and heartaches of the homosexual. Men and women, many of whom were caught up in what they thought to be the same "hopeless" condition, are now *completely free* in Christ and *dedicated to helping others* experience that same freedom. Their address is:

EXODUS INTERNATIONAL
P.O. BOX 2121
SAN RAFAEL, CA 94912
Phone: (415) 454-1017

They have plenty of written material, and they can get you in touch with a ministry in your area that will listen and be completely confidential—people that can help you get free.

## ▶ ONE FINAL NOTE

Just as much as God hates the act of homosexuality, He hates the prejudice and contempt that so many people have against the homosexual. God expects all His children to have love and compassion for those trapped in sin.

Remember, homosexuals are not the enemy. They are hurt and battered prisoners of the enemy. And our job is to help free them.

# WHAT IS GOD REALLY LIKE?

▶ To know what God is really like we don't have too much to go on besides what the Bible says. I mean, it's not like He does guest spots on the Tonight Show or you can whip out your billfold and look at His latest snapshot. But the Bible does a pretty good job in describing Him. In fact if you were to list just the passages that explain what God is like, you'd wind up with a book over twice the size of this one.

*So, what is He like? I mean, are we talking "Wizard of Oz" time with the booming voice and puffs of smoke, or is he some white-bearded old duffer shuffling around, or what? Does He really have a personality? Or is He just some cosmic force that is everywhere and in everything?*

God has personality—a very definite personality. He has specific likes and dislikes—things that please Him and things that peeve Him. He has character traits that you'd expect to see only in an infinite Being, and others that you can find in the guy next door.

## ▶ THE UNIQUE QUALITIES

God has some characteristics that are His and His alone. For instance, He's . . .

### INFINITE

He was not created. He never had a beginning; He'll never have an end. Scripture is pretty clear about the matter:

> How great is God—beyond our understanding! The number of His years is past finding out.
>
> Job 36:26

> Before the mountains were born or You brought forth the earth and the world, from everlasting to everlasting You are God.
>
> Psalm 90:2

And while we're talking about infinite, how about size?

> Even the highest heaven cannot contain You.
>
> 1 Kings 8:27

> "Do not I fill heaven and earth?" declares the Lord.
>
> Jeremiah 23:24

## THE CREATOR

The fact that God created all things probably doesn't come as too great a shock to you. But for some it's a bit of a surprise to learn that it wasn't God the Father who did the creating—it was His Son. In a few pages we'll cover more on how Jesus fits into the God picture, but for now take a look at what Scripture says about His creative abilities:

> For by Him [Jesus] all things were created: things in heaven and on earth, visible and invisible, whether thrones or powers or rulers or authorities; all things were created by Him and for Him.
>
> Colossians 1:16

> In these last days He has spoken to us by His Son, whom He appointed heir of all things, and through whom He made the universe.
>
> Hebrews 1:2

## THE SUPREME BOSS

God is the One in charge; no one even runs a close second.

> Yours, O Lord, is the greatness and the power and the glory and the majesty and the splendor, for everything in heaven and earth is Yours. Yours, O Lord, is the kingdom; You are exalted as head over all. Wealth and honor come from You; You are the ruler of

all things. In Your hands are strength and power to exalt and give strength to all.

1 Chronicles 29:11-12

## ALL-KNOWING

The eyes of the Lord are everywhere.

Proverbs 15:3

Nothing in all creation is hidden from God's sight. Everything is uncovered and laid bare before the eyes of Him to whom we must give account.

Hebrews 4:13

## ALL-POWERFUL

With God all things are possible.

Matthew 19:26

For nothing is impossible with God.

Luke 1:37

## UNCHANGING

Now this has an up side and a down side. The good news is that in this frantic, ever changing world of ours—where what's in this morning is out this evening, where promises are made to be broken, where relationships are as disposable as Kleenex—it's great to know God will always stay unshakable in His integrity, honesty, and faithfulness.

I the Lord do not change.

Malachi 3:6

God is not a man, that He should lie,
nor a son of man, that He should
change His mind.

Numbers 23:19

But this also means that God's principles and
standards won't be dictated by the latest trends
and whims; even at the risk of being "uncool,"
God will stay the same. He would rather be uncool than be unfaithful.

Unfortunately that often makes His standards
(and followers) seem outdated. But it's a small
price to pay since, as we've already discussed, His
methods wind up being the best anyway.

## HOLY

God is so pure and intensely good that no one
can even stand in His presence. In fact when He
came down to talk with Moses on top of Mount
Sinai, He warned the people not even to touch
the mountain or they'd die (Exodus 19:12).

Whew.

Another time over 50,000 men were struck
dead by looking into the ark (where God's presence dwelt). The remaining survivors probably
put it best when they said:

Who can stand in the presence of the
Lord, this holy God?

1 Samuel 6:20

It's as if God is this incredibly pure goodness,
this intense perfection that vaporizes any imper-
fection that comes close to Him. That's why the
cleansing power of Jesus' blood is so important.

Without Jesus to take all of our imperfections upon Himself, we could never approach God—much less live to tell about it.

### ▶ WHAT DOES HE LOOK LIKE?

A good question. Because of God's holiness it's pretty hard to tell. In fact it's because of this holiness that those who have gotten close to Him can describe only this incredibly intense light.

> God, the blessed and only Ruler, the King of kings and Lord of lords, who alone is immortal and who lives in un-approachable light, whom no one has seen or can see.
>
> 1 Timothy 6:15-16

Oh, there is one person who has seen God—sort of. It happened to Moses, and it's one of my favorite accounts in the Old Testament.

As Moses and God were becoming better and better friends, Moses began asking if it was possible to see Him. He wasn't asking out of doubt or curiosity. He was asking out of love. Here was a guy who was really getting close to God's heart, and he just wanted to know what his Friend looked like. It was a touching request that must have really moved God. But God's response is equally as moving.

First He explains the hard reality:

> You cannot see My face, for no one may see Me and live.
>
> Exodus 33:20

But then, out of a tender love and compassion for His friend, God comes up with a solution.

> There is a place near Me where you may stand on a rock. When My glory passes by, I will put you in a cleft in the rock and cover you with My hand until I have passed by. Then I will remove My hand and you will see My back; but My face must not be seen.
>
> Exodus 33:21-23

What a perfect picture—a perfect blending of God's holiness and His love.

## ▶ GOD'S LOVE

"God is love." We've all heard it a million times, and it's definitely biblical. But since the word *love* is tossed around so carelessly these days, let's see what it really means when it refers to God.

### PATIENCE

> He is not easily angered; He is full of kindness, and anxious not to punish you.
>
> Joel 1:13 (TLB)

### MERCY AND GRACE

> But God is so rich in mercy; He loved us so much that even though we were spiritually dead and doomed by our sins, He gave us back our lives again when He raised Christ from the dead—

only by His undeserved favor have we ever been saved—and lifted us up from the grave into glory along with Christ, where we sit with Him in the heavenly realms—all because of what Christ Jesus did.

Ephesians 2:4-6 (TLB)

## FAITHFULNESS

The Old Testament hero Joshua spent an entire lifetime trusting God. As Joshua prepared to die, he had this to say about God's unfailing faithfulness:

You know with all your heart and soul that not one of all the good promises the Lord your God gave you has failed. Every promise has been fulfilled; not one has failed.

Joshua 23:14

And the Lord Himself gave this promise:

The heavens will vanish like smoke, the earth will wear out like a garment and its inhabitants die like flies. But My salvation will last forever, My righteousness will never fail.

Isaiah 51:6

## PROTECTOR AND DEFENDER

"For the eyes of the Lord are on the righteous and His ears are attentive to their prayer, but the face of the Lord is against those who do evil." Who is go-

ing to harm you if you are eager to do
good?

1 Peter 3:12-13

Are not two sparrows sold for a penny?
Yet not one of them will fall to the
ground apart from the will of your Father. And even the very hairs of your
head are all numbered. So don't be
afraid; you are worth more than many
sparrows.

Matthew 10:29-31

## PROVIDER

So do not worry, saying, "What shall
we eat?" or "What shall we drink?" or
"What shall we wear?" For the pagans
run after all these things, and your
Heavenly Father knows that you need
them. But seek first His kingdom and
His righteousness, and all these things
will be given to you as well.

Matthew 6:31-33

## GUIDE

The Lord will guide you always.

Isaiah 58:11

## SAVIOUR

For God so loved the world that He
gave His one and only Son, that whoever believes in Him shall not perish
but have eternal life. For God did not

send His Son into the world to con-
demn the world, but to save the world
through Him.

John 3:16-17

## ▶ *TOUGHER QUALITIES*

But God's no wimp. There's a tougher side to
Him too. Qualities such as:

### WRATH

Wrath can be defined as "justifiable anger." And if
anyone's got a right to be hot under the collar, I
figure it's God. I mean, look how people treat
Him, His commands, His world, and His loved
ones.

Because of His mercy and patience, He's been
holding back His wrath. But it won't be that way
forever. The Apostle John, who took a sight-see-
ing tour into heaven and the future, put what he
saw this way:

> Then the kings of the earth, the
> princes, the generals, the rich, the
> mighty, and every slave and every free
> man hid in caves and among the rocks
> of the mountains. They called to the
> mountains and the rocks, "Fall on us
> and hide us from the face of Him who
> sits on the throne and from the wrath
> of the Lamb [Jesus]! For the great day
> of Their wrath has come, and who can
> stand?

Revelation 6:15-17

## JEALOUSY

And for those who think God really doesn't care who you worship, there are these words:

> Do not worship any other god, for the Lord, whose name is Jealous, is a jealous God.
>
> Exodus 34:14

> They made Him jealous with their foreign gods and angered Him with their detestable idols.
>
> Deuteronomy 32:16

## ▶ THE TRINITY

Finally, no discussion about God can be complete without mentioning the Trinity. Over and over again the Scripture makes it clear that "the Lord is one" (Deuteronomy 6:4). OK, fine, no problem.

But there are plenty of other Scriptures that talk about the Holy Spirit being God, about Jesus Christ being God, and about the Father being God. So what gives? How many do we have here? Will the real God please stand up?

It's true, we do have one God. But He exists in three distinct Persons. Confusing? You bet. We don't have anything in our own human experience to compare Him with. But the Scriptures clearly identify these three Persons—just as clearly as they tell us that God is one.

> Let *Us* make man in *Our* image, in *Our* likeness.
>
> Genesis 1:26

> Therefore go and make disciples of all
> nations, baptizing them in the name of
> the *Father* and of the *Son* and of the
> *Holy Spirit*.
>
> Matthew 28:19

In fact all three Persons of the Trinity made a special appearance (or at least were heard) on the occasion of Jesus' baptism:

> As soon as Jesus was baptized, He went
> up out of the water. At that moment
> heaven was opened, and He saw the
> Spirit of God descending like a dove
> and lighting on Him. And a voice from
> heaven said, "This is my Son, whom I
> love; with Him I am well pleased."
>
> Matthew 3:16-17

## ▶ THE BEST PICTURE

If you're having problems putting together all that we've said about God, then just go ahead and picture Jesus Christ.

> He is the image of the invisible God,
> the firstborn over all creation. For by
> Him all things were created: things in
> heaven and on earth, visible and invisi-
> ble . . . all things were created by Him
> and for Him. He is before all things,
> and in Him all things hold together.
> . . . For God was pleased to have *all*
> His fullness dwell in Him."
>
> Colossians 1:15-17, 19

# EVOLUTION AND CREATION

▶ you're thinking you'll finally be able to shut down your biology teacher with this chapter or you'll finally be able to convince so-and-so that there's a God, think again.

For starters, your biology teacher will have far more info than I can squeeze into these puny few pages (though I'll list some books in the end that will give him or her a run for the money).

Second, the information in this chapter is not for you to beat anybody over the head with. (Not even all Christians agree on just what happened when God created the world.) This chapter is only a quick summary of what many Christians believe about Creation and evolution. It's written to encourage *you* in *your* faith, to show you that Christians can and do respond to challenges about what we believe.

## WHO CARES?
*What difference does it make what I believe about evolution or Creation?*

A good question. But if the Bible can't be trusted in what it says about Creation, then maybe it can't be trusted in what it says about Jesus. And if what it says about Jesus can't be trusted, then you and I may be the brunt of the world's biggest practical joke.

The good news is that the Bible *can* be trusted. In fact, a growing number of scientists believe that there is more scientific data supporting belief in Creation than supporting the theory of evolution.

## ▶ THE SECOND LAW OF THERMODYNAMICS

The Second Law of Thermodynamics is a primary building block of science—a major law by which the entire universe functions. It rates right up there with gravity and all the biggies. The Second Law of Thermodynamics states that everything goes from a state of order to disorder. Rocks erode, stars burn out, iron rusts, people grow old and die. In other words, no matter what it is, if it's in our universe, in one way or another it's eventually going to fall apart. Or as Isaac Asimov puts it, "As far as we know, all changes are in the direction of . . . increasing disorder, of increasing randomness, of running down" ("Can Decreasing Entropy Exist in the Universe?" Science Digest, May 1973, p. 76, as quoted by *Science Says No!* Creation Science Society).

**43**

And yet full-scale evolution teaches just the opposite. It teaches that somehow, some way in this decaying universe, the building blocks of life have decided to break this most basic rule and head in the opposite direction—instead of going from complex to simple, they magically went from simple to complex.

An interesting idea, but one that can't fly—at least not in our universe.

▶ *HOW OLD?*

Evolutionists claim that the earth is 4 to 5 billion years old. Many Christians believe the Bible indicates that it's 6 to 10 *thousand* years old. Big difference. Here is some of the evidence that leads many people to support the idea of a 6- to 10-thousand-year-old earth.

MOON DUST

Back when man was getting ready to traipse about on the moon, there were some hefty worries by the evolutionists about his fate. Harold Hill put it best:

> When NASA began planning for our first moon walk, much concern was expressed over the "fact" that the layer of dust covering the moon might swallow up the first astronaut who landed there. Evolutionists insisted that due to the large volume of dust being dumped on that heavenly body each year, based on the 14,300,000 tons es-

timated to be falling annually on planet earth (*Scientific American*, February 1960, p. 132), after 5 billion years (their estimate of the age of the moon), the coating of dust on the moon would be 137 feet deep! (See Kofahl & Segraves, *The Creation Explanation* [Wheaton, Ill.: Harold Shaw Publishers] pp. 190, 195.)

Just how deep was the moon dust as reported by Astronaut Neil Armstrong? Just about one-eighth of an inch. (*From Goo to You by Way of the Zoo*, Fleming H. Revell, p. 132)

This tiny amount of dust suggests to many scientists that the moon has been around less than 10,000 years!

*OK, so the moon's age fits in with the Creation story. But what about the earth's age?*

## OIL

As we know, oil can be under intense pressure when it's in the ground, which explains why it shoots high into the air as a "gusher" when it's first released. But if the earth is as old as evolutionists believe, then that pressure should not even exist.

Let me explain. The type of rocks that usually surround oil reserves are "absorbent" enough that, over the millions of years, the pressure should have easily worked its way through them. Or, as Jolly F. Griggs says:

Studies of the permeability of the rocks surrounding an oil reservoir show that any pressure built up should be bled off in surrounding rocks within a few thousand years. The excessive pressures found within oil beds argues for a youthful age of less than 10,000 years. (*Science Says No!* p. 24)

## MAGNETIC FIELD

Scientists have found that the magnetic field of the earth decays 50 percent every 1,400 years. This means that 1,400 years ago the magnetic field was two times stronger than today, 2,800 years ago it was four times stronger, and so on.

*So?*

So, with all this magnetic energy, if the earth were only 30,000 years old (not to mention 5 billion), it would have suffered a massive meltdown. A more probable age? Glad you asked. According to Dr. Henry Morris, "10,000 years seems to be an outside limit for the age of the earth, based on the present decay of its magnetic field" (*Scientific Creationism,* Master Books, p. 158).

There's more information pointing to a younger earth, such as the amount of helium 4 that should have escaped from the crust into the atmosphere, or the amount of elements that should have been dumped into the ocean from the rivers, and the list goes on—but I think you get the picture.

## ▶ *FOSSILS*

If life evolved slowly from the simplest form to the most complex, then there should be plenty of fossils to prove it. As the animals die off and are imbedded in the sediments, we should see the history of their gradual change. We should see fossils of animals slowly evolving from eels to fish to frogs to lizards to birds to monkeys to man.

And what have we found?

> There is not a single, indisputable transitional creature bridging a gap between the categories listed above. The millions of missing links are still missing. (*Science Says No!* p. 17)

> There is not the slightest evidence that any of the major groups of animals arose from each other. Each is a special animal complex . . . appearing, therefore, as a special distinct creation. (Austin H. Clark, U.S. Museum of Natural History, in *The New Evolution: Zoogenesis,* pp. 189–196 as quoted in *From Goo to You by Way of the Zoo,* p. 120)

Or, as one discouraged scientist put it:

> My attempt to demonstrate evolution by an experiment carried on for more than forty years, has completely failed. . . . The fossil material is now so complete that . . . the lack of transitional series cannot be explained as

due to the scarcity of the material. The deficiencies are real, they will never be filled. The idea of evolution rests on pure belief [as opposed to scientific fact]! (Herbert Nilsson, Director of Botany Institute, Lund University, in *Synthetische Artbildung,* Vol. I & II, 1953 [trans.] as quoted in *From Goo to You by Way of the Zoo,* p. 120)

*But what about all those ape-man fossils they've found?*

A good question. According to Jolly F. Griggs, there are no fossil transitions between men and apes. About the fossils that have been found, he says:

The scholarship in this area leaves much to be desired.

*Piltdown Man* was a candidate for half-man and half-ape status for 40 years and as recently as the 50's before it was discovered to be a cruel hoax. Over 500 doctoral theses were written about these bones. . . .

*Nebraska Man* and his family were reconstructed on the basis of a single tooth. It turned out to be a tooth of an extinct pig.

*Java Man* consisted of bones of both apes and humans found over 50 feet apart and were judged to belong to one individual. The discovery also found skulls and bones of modern humans in the same gravels but hid them so as not to "confuse the situation." . . .

*Peking Man* was promoted for a while. Some thought he was man. Some thought he was an animal hunted by man. In any case the actual bones were conveniently lost. . . . Only hand-carved models remain and they differ in many respects with descriptions of the skulls written by reputable scientists. (*Science Says No!* p. 18)

*OK, so maybe there aren't any missing links. But doesn't the fossil record show that the farther down you go into the rocks, the lower the life form you find—you know, like trilobites being buried a lot farther down than human fossils?*

If the theory of evolution were true, you would definitely expect that to be the case. But over and over and over again, the fossils of plants and animals that were supposed to have lived millions of years from one another have been found side by side.

## WHAT ABOUT CARBON DATING?

Carbon dating and other systems are reliable *only* if the earth's atmosphere and magnetic fields were stable or were similar to what we know them to be today (a prospect that's not too likely). The best example of the potential for error is probably the live mollusk that was carbon-14 dated to be 3,000 years old!

## ▶ GENETICS
### HYBRIDS

Those of you that live on a farm know how hybrids can improve crop production. By "cross-breeding," as it were, we can wind up with heartier plants, greater yield, even a tastier product. Isn't this proof of gradual evolution?

Not quite. Quoting again from Harold Hill:

> Actually, hybrids *disprove* evolution, because the seed of the hybrid does not reproduce the parent plant but the grandparents. Unless mechanically pollinated, the seed of the hybrid *cannot* reproduce its own kind. The hybridizing has to be done all over again for each season and every generation. (*From Goo to You by Way of the Zoo,* p. 140, italics added)

The same can be said for animals. Take a look at the mule. A cross between a horse and a donkey, he makes a great worker. But, like all hybrids, he cannot reproduce—he's sterile. It's hard for a species to evolve if it can't reproduce.

### NATURAL SELECTION AND MUTANTS

To survive and keep fitting in with their changing environment, animals can make all sorts of little adaptations. A well-known example is the peppered moth in England which actually changed its color from light to dark so it could blend better into the tree trunks that were being blackened from all the pollution. This adaptation is a wonderful little side benefit for living organisms and shows the care in which they were created.

But that moth will always remain a moth. Its genetic code makes it impossible to switch or develop into something else. It will change as much as a moth can change to survive, but it will always be a moth. And if it cannot survive as a moth, then its fate will be the same as all the other plants and animals that have died out.

You'd think that since every living organism is so determined to survive, we would have seen at *least one* incident of evolution take place.

Not so.

> It is significant that not one new species of plant or animal is known to have evolved on Earth during recorded history, but large numbers have become extinct. (*Scientific Creationism,* p. 58)

We've barely scratched the surface of this topic, but I hope these few facts have helped a little. Remember, they are not to be used as debating tools. No one is ever won to Christ by losing an argument. They are won by people sharing His love. This information is simply to demonstrate that you can be a Christian without committing mental suicide.

If you're interested in more thorough and detailed info let me strongly recommend:

*Scientific Creationism*
Dr. Henry Morris
Master Books, El Cajon, Calif.

Or, for a little lighter reading:

> *From Goo to You by Way of the Zoo*
> Harold Hill with Irene Burk Harrell and
> Mary Elizabeth Rogers
> Fleming H. Revell Company, Old Tappan,
> N.J.

For guest speakers, newsletters, books, tapes, or videos there's a group of top-notch scientists you may want to contact the people at the:

> Institute for Creation Research
> P.O. Box 2667
> El Cajon, CA 92021

# SURVIVING DEVOTIONAL TIME

▶ *Does spending time with God always have to be a cure for insomnia? Is there any way to do it that's interesting? And really, is it even that necessary?*

Good questions. Let's see if we can come up with some answers.

Back in the first century, one of the religious hotshots thought he was going to corner Jesus by asking, "Of all these laws which is the most important?"

Jesus' answer?

> Love the Lord your God with all your heart and with all your soul and with all your mind. This is the first and greatest commandment.
>
> Matthew 22:37-38

*But how? I mean, honestly, how can we love someone we've never even seen? We barely know Him, so how can we love Him?*

The answer:

We can't. It's absolutely impossible to love someone (even God) until we get to know him. And the only way to get to know somebody is through . . .

## COMMUNICATION

If I were to run out into the street and ask the first girl I met to marry me, she'd probably die laughing. She wouldn't even know me, let alone love me.

So how would we take care of that? We'd communicate. She'd talk, I'd listen. I'd talk, she'd listen. And gradually, as we got to know each other and if we were the right match, we'd fall in love.

The same is true with God and us. How can we love Him if we don't really know Him? And how can we know Him without communicating—without listening, without talking?

## ▶ *LISTENING*

For those of us who don't have a direct phone line to God, the usual way of listening to Him is to read His Word, the Bible.

There is something unique and powerful about the Word—something supernatural. For starters, it was with His Word that God created the universe: "And God said . . . and it was."

That's all. He just spoke His words and *bingo,*

instant universe. Pretty impressive. But there's more proof of the power of God's Word.

Remember when Satan and Jesus were battling it out on the Mount of Temptation—when the most evil force in the universe was trying to destroy the Creator of the universe? They didn't use guns, bombs, or missiles. They didn't even try to nuke each other. Instead, these two knew the most powerful force in Creation and they used it on each other again and again and again. Their choice?

God's Holy Word.

*But what makes it so powerful?*

According to 2 Timothy 3:16, the Bible is "God-breathed." So even though writing it down involved many different people over many, many years, it's all right from God's mouth. No wonder it carries such a punch.

And there's more. The Word is so powerful that when we expose ourselves to it we actually get changed. It actually . . .
- cleanses us (Ephesians 5:26),
- enables us to see what we're really like (James 1:23-25),
- encourages us (Romans 15:4),
- equips us to do good (2 Timothy 3:17),
- leads us to faith (Romans 10:17),
- shows us the way to be saved (James 1:21).

Not a bad deal. And it does all of the above *plus* help us get to know God.

*But if it's so important, how come so much of it's so boring?*

Another good question. But maybe the problem isn't so much with *what* we're reading as in *how* we're reading it.

## ▶ HOW TO READ

I have to admit that when I read the Bible there are times my mind is on everything but what I'm reading. But because I've seen the tremendous change reading it has made in my life, I tough it out. I nudge my mind back to the page and continue. In fact because there have been so many positive changes in me from reading His Word, I try never to let a day slip by without reading a little.

It may not always be fun—I'm not crazy about eating vegetables either—but I know, just as I need those vegetables for my body, I need His Word for my soul.

Reading the Bible may not always be fun, but I tell you in all honesty: *the gain is a million times worth the pain.*

But to help make it a little more enjoyable, let me share a few pointers I've stumbled on.

**1.** Don't begin in Genesis and think you'll plow all the way through. There are sections in the Old Testament that lose even the most dedicated. Instead, start off with one of the Gospels or one of the New Testament letters. Then gradually, once you get the hang of it, start slipping into the Old Testament, maybe with Proverbs or the Psalms.

**2.** Don't try to read massive quantities in one setting. Instead, read just a little bit, chewing on it thoroughly before moving on. I find a chapter a day is about it for me. And because I don't turn it into a marathon session, I'm not nearly as reluctant to sit down the next day.

3. Pray. Ask God, "How does this apply to me? Why did You spend time writing this and why are You having me spend time reading it?" Basically, "What are You trying to teach me?"

4. Get a version you can read! There are a lot out there—everything from the *Living Bible* (which I read to my young daughter) to the *King James* (which I barely understand). The best I've found for high schoolers and young adults is the new *NIV Student Bible*.

5. Get some help. There's quite a bit of information incorporated in the Scriptures—information that doesn't always make as much sense on first reading now as it did 2,000 years ago. So you might want to pick up a commentary that helps explain what you're reading. There're a few of us out there that write commentaries just for teens, making the Bible relevant and readable for you. If you want, give us a shot.

Anyway, these are just a few pointers that will make your reading a little easier and enjoyable. But whatever you do, if you haven't started reading on a regular basis, begin today. Nothing will have as great an impact on your life. Let me repeat:

*NOTHING WILL HAVE AS GREAT AN IMPACT ON YOUR LIFE.*

And nothing will draw you as close to God as listening to Him on a regular basis.

## ▶ *TALKING*

The other half of communicating with God is talking (praying). But, if you're anything like most of us, you're good for about 30 seconds before the old mind starts worrying about that upcoming test, the fight you had with your best friend, or how you're going to con Mom and Dad into letting you off restriction for the game this Friday.

But since He created us, God has a pretty good idea where our weaknesses are, including when it comes to our trying to pray. That's why He gave us an example to follow, an outline on how to pray.

### THE LORD'S PRAYER

Now many of us know about the Lord's prayer; maybe you've even recited it since you were a little tyke. But did you know Jesus didn't give it to us to recite? Instead, when He gave it to us He said, "This is *how* you should pray," not "This is *what* you should pray." He was giving us an example, a model to follow—not a bunch of words to rattle off.

So, when I pray, I try to follow His outline. That way if my mind drifts off or I lose my place, I know right where to come back to—while at the same time making sure I cover the areas *He* feels are important.

Basically the example He's given us is divided into five sections. The first being:

"OUR FATHER IN HEAVEN,

HALLOWED BE YOUR NAME."

This is the praise section of my prayer: "hallowed (honored, worshiped, revered, adored) be Your name." It's interesting that God encourages us to start off our time with Him by praising and glorifying Him.

*Why?*

Probably because that's what we were originally created for in the first place. So praise basically just gets us in sync with our original purpose.

Praise also breaks through the wall that so many of us feel is between God and ourselves. Praise somehow throws open the door and allows us into His presence. That's probably why the psalm orders us to . . .

> Enter His gates with thanksgiving and
> His courts with praise.

> Psalm 100:4

*How? I mean, people always say to worship God and praise Him. So what do we do, just sit around and say, "Thank you, thank you," a bunch of times or what?*

There are no hard, fast rules to worshiping. But I'll tell you how I do it.

Usually I'll start off by singing a song that's directed right to God and that tells Him how great I think He is. Then I'll pick a slower, more peaceful song and gradually quiet and silence my mind. At last I'll sit very, very still and think about a specific goodness of Jesus—His mercy, His love, His faithfulness, His provision, even His name. And almost before I know it, I've entered

His presence. I'll start to feel His peace, His joy.

Sometimes I'll whisper His praises; sometimes I'll just sit silently basking in His presence. That still doesn't mean my mind won't wander. But when it does, I just gently direct it back to the Lord.

Eventually I may pick up my Bible and quietly read a psalm of worship *to Him*—slowly, with great feeling. Other times I may sing another hymn, or quietly recite words describing His majesty, or dwell on His holiness or on how good He's been to me. Exactly what I do doesn't matter. What really matters is that I'm worshiping and experiencing my Creator.

*What if I'm bummed or don't feel like praising? Won't that make me like a hypocrite?*

We have to remember that praise is not based on feelings. Praise is based on OBEDIENCE *not* EMOTION. Over and over again the Bible commands us to offer up a "*sacrifice* of thanksgiving." (I don't know about you, but sacrifice isn't something I'm always crazy about "offering up.") But if I obey, if I find the tiniest of things to start thanking and praising God for, the feeling usually follows. (And if it doesn't, I've obeyed anyway, and that in itself should be enough.)

Once we're in God's presence, it's time to move on to Phase II.

"YOUR KINGDOM COME,
YOUR WILL BE DONE
ON EARTH AS IT IS IN HEAVEN."

By "Your kingdom come," we're not necessarily asking for heaven to suddenly drop down from the clouds. But we are asking for Jesus' rulership, His power and authority to take over various areas of our lives.

"Your kingdom be established more strongly in my heart, in this area of my life, in that habit I can't seem to shake, in my relationship with so-and-so, in my grades, in my getting on the team, in my parents' getting along."

And . . .

"Your perfect will be done in each of those situations—don't let Satan have his way; don't let other people have theirs; don't even let me have mine. If you have something better planned, then please step in there and do it. Your will be done. Make it happen *Your* way."

*So why pray if God's just going to do His will anyway?*

Well for one thing, God wants us to. He makes that perfectly clear in Scripture. When we obey His command for us to pray to Him, we indicate *our* willingness to go along with *His* will. And more often than not, when we pray for God to work something out as He sees fit, we find ourselves being the tools He chooses to use to do it.

So, praying for His will does two things. First, it makes it clear that we want Him to call the shots. Second, it allows us the privilege of becoming partners with Him in whatever He does do.

"GIVE US TODAY OUR DAILY BREAD.
Or . . .

"Please provide my needs today. Please help me get the money to get my car out of the shop, to take Jenny to the prom, to pay my rent, to eat."

Interesting that Jesus doesn't say, "Give us today our monthly bread" or "our yearly bread." Instead He makes it clear that God will provide *as* we have need—and not necessarily before. It's as if He wants us to have a little faith on a daily basis instead of getting everything in advance so we can forget about Him.

"FORGIVE US OUR DEBTS, AS WE ALSO
HAVE FORGIVEN OUR DEBTORS."

Hmmm. It seems that if I haven't forgiven somebody, I might be in for a little unforgiveness myself.

When I come to this portion of my prayer-time, I always do a little inventory to see if there's somebody I'm holding a grudge against. If I do have a grudge, I'll get rid of it (usually praying for the person's success is a good method). But one way or another, I make sure I'm no longer bitter or unforgiving.

Once that's taken care of, I ask God to forgive me for all my foul-ups (accidental or intentional) and trust that Jesus' sacrifice on that cross is greater than any sin I could have dreamed up.

"LEAD US NOT INTO TEMPTATION,
BUT DELIVER US FROM THE EVIL ONE.

Finally, I ask God to help me out in any weakness I have: lust, lying, cheating, favoritism, gossip, booze, dope, putting people down—whatever area I may be struggling with. I ask that the Lord will keep me from situations that I don't think I can completely handle.

And if for some reason He doesn't keep me from them, then I ask that He'll give me the strength to get through them.

## ALL THIS TO SAY . . .

If we really want to love God, then it's a good idea to get to know Him. And the only way we can get to know Him is by communicating—reading and praying.

If you haven't made this a regular, day-to-day routine, then there's no time like the present to start. Try just 10, 15, 20 minutes a day. Usually the last thing at night or the first thing in the morning is best. But whenever you do it, *do it*.

*Nothing* will make a greater impact on your life than communicating with the Creator on a regular basis—absolutely nothing.

# WHY DO GOOD PEOPLE SUFFER?

▶ I was barely out of high school when my folks told me that they were getting a divorce. Talk about emotional devastation. I was a wreck. Our home was split apart, the love and security of my family was ripped away, even the house that we had built on property that we had cleared with our own hands was eventually sold to total strangers. Suddenly everything in my life that seemed safe and good was gone.

Well, almost everything. At least I had the girl I'd dated for three years and was planning on marrying. Amidst all of the turmoil I knew I could still count on her. She was my only security and the only thing I had left. Then, less than six weeks after my folks broke their news, she had some news of her own—she was in love with another guy.

I have never experienced such pain, such anguish. Hit me with a car, give me a couple of broken arms—physical pain would have been a blessing compared to the emotional torment I was going through. (Of course now, when I look back, this seems like small potatoes compared to world hunger or terminal cancer, but you couldn't have convinced me of that then.)

I remember the hurt was so intense that there were times I could barely breathe. I remember begging God to take the pain away or, better yet, to take my life. And through the tears, the sleeplessness, and the aimless wanderings in the middle of the night, I kept asking the question *WHY?*

*What had I done to deserve this? I hadn't killed anybody, hadn't robbed any banks, hadn't beaten up any babies. I mean, I was a Christian, for crying out loud! So why, why, if You love me, are You torturing me???*

It's taken nearly 15 years, but I finally found my answer.

## ▶ WHY PAIN?

In his excellent book *Where Is God When it Hurts?* (Zondervan), Philip Yancey insists that some types of pain are a gift. And he's right. Without pain we wouldn't know if our hand was resting on a hot stove (until we started smelling smoke). Without pain we might keep hammering our thumb instead of the nail. Without pain we wouldn't even know if there was something wrong with our body that needed fixing.

And in case you still think life without pain

would be some sort of gift from heaven, Yancey goes on to describe a condition where people are actually blessed with such a gift, where they actually lose the ability to feel pain. Its name? Leprosy.

When leprosy strikes, parts of the body go numb. I use to think that all those fingerless hands and leg stumps were because leprosy had rotted off those parts of the body. Not true. Those parts had simply lost their ability to feel pain. And, over the years, the patients had slowly worn out, infected, or broken them off. Why? Because the patients didn't know they were injuring those parts. They no longer had any type of warning system. They no longer could feel pain.

For them, this inability to feel pain was no blessing. Instead, it was a terrible curse.

## ▶ BUT DOES PAIN HAVE TO HURT?

Philip Yancey talks about various warning systems that doctors have tried to use in place of pain. You know, systems that would stimulate other senses instead of our pain center—senses like sight or hearing. But the results were ineffective:

> The signal was not unpleasant enough. A patient would tolerate a loud noise if he wanted to do something such as turn a screwdriver too hard, even though the signal told him it could be harmful [to his hand]. Blinking lights were tried and eliminated for the same

re son. Brand [the head doctor] finally resorted to electric shock to make people let go of something that might hurt them. People had to be *forced* to remove their hands. . . . The stimulus had to be unpleasant, just as pain is unpleasant. *(Where Is God When It Hurts?* p. 28)

So in many ways pain actually is a type of gift. Without it, we would literally destroy our bodies.

## ▶ WHAT ABOUT OTHER TYPES OF SUFFERING?
*Hunger, disease, war, murders—what about that type of stuff?*

First, keep in mind that these types of suffering were not in God's original plan. Remember the Garden of Eden with all its happiness? That's what He originally intended for us—not the pain, suffering, and death we have today.

But because we insisted on doing things our way, we invited sin into this world, and with sin came all its pain, suffering, and death. Suffering is a natural result and warning sign that something is wrong with our world (sin) just as physical pain is a natural result and warning sign that something is wrong with our body.

Without sin there would only be love and respect—no violence, no murders, no war.

Without sin there would be enough love and sharing so nobody would be starving or in need.

Without the abuse of sin on our bodies they

would never have become so vulnerable to sickness and disease.

And without sin, God would not have had to introduce death. (He brought it in as a relief so we wouldn't have to endure the sufferings of our sinful world for eternity.)

*But couldn't God have made us so we wouldn't sin?*

Sure. He could have made us into mindless little robots that would always love Him and always do exactly what He said. But the only problem is that we wouldn't have any freedom. We'd have no choice. We'd be like some battery-powered doll that, whenever you pressed the button, would automatically say, "I love you."

What a joke. That's not love. And love is what God wants—a real, honest-to-goodness love relationship, not some programmed computer response. God wants us to love Him because *we* want to love Him—plain and simple. If He wanted mindless, wind-up toys, He could have created them.

## ▶ BUT WHY DOES IT HAPPEN TO GOOD PEOPLE?

There is probably no more haunting question in the world than this one. In the Old Testament the entire book of Job is devoted to this one thought. Let's take a look at what it says.

The Bible calls Job "the greatest man among the people of the East." In fact, on more than one occasion God Himself referred to Job as "blameless and upright, a man who fears God and shuns evil" (Job 1:8, 2:3). And yet God allowed Satan to destroy all of Job's livestock (11,000 head), his servants, every one of his 10 children, and to strike down Job himself with painful boils from head to foot.

Talk about intense. But why? What did Job do to deserve such suffering? Was it because, as his friends kept suggesting, he was being punished for something he did wrong? Hardly. God Himself said Job was blameless.

So what gives? Was God trying to teach him something?

If He was, He never bothered telling Job.

Was He trying to get Job to work up a bunch of faith so he could get healed?

Nope. According to the Bible, the guy already loved and believed God with his whole heart.

Was it because God had forgotten?

No way. Chapters 1 and 2 are full of God's talking about the guy.

So why?

Again, the answer comes back to God's wanting sincere love.

Satan kept telling God that He wasn't really giving Job a choice. He kept saying that the only reason Job loved the Lord was because He kept blessing him. In essence he accused God of buying Job's love—instead of giving the man a free choice to make up his own mind.

What was the Lord's response to Satan? "Do with him as you please, only spare his life" (Job 2:6, TLB). And Satan did just that!

I wonder how often in our own suffering God

is simply purifying our love for Him. How often is He proving to us and the rest of the universe that our love for Him doesn't have to depend on things or circumstances or on getting our own way? True love is not something that has to be bribed or bought; it can become something that is true and deep and eternal—no matter what happens.

## ▶ OTHER REASONS

Besides purifying our love, there are three other reasons that God allows good people to suffer.

### TO DISCIPLINE US

> Our fathers disciplined us for a little while as they thought best; but God disciplines us for our good, that we may share in His holiness. No discipline seems pleasant at the time, but painful. Later on, however, it produces a harvest of righteousness and peace for those who have been trained by it.
>                                Hebrews 12:10-11

I almost hesitate to bring this up since discipline is the first thing everyone always points to. *I wonder why that happened to so-and-so? He must really be out of line.* Or, *God, why are you doing this to me? What am I doing that's so wrong?*

Now it's true that, if there's something out of sync in your life, God may indeed be using some form of trial or hardship to get your attention and let you know He's not fooling around. And, like the pain from touching a hot stove, it may not be pleasant—for the time being. But in the long run you'll be happier for a little pain now than for burning flesh later.

But remember: this is only one of several ways the Lord uses suffering. Be *very careful* not to jump to this conclusion too often about yourself—and especially about other people.

## TO COMFORT OTHERS

Another reason we suffer is so we can help others who have or will be going through similar situations. As the Apostle Paul said to his friends:

> If we are distressed, it is for your comfort and salvation; if we are comforted, it is for your comfort.
>
> 2 Corinthians 1:6

It's one thing to cruise up in your limo to a suffering person, roll down your tinted glass window, and shout, "Hey, where's your faith, Scum? If you really believed, God would help you." But it's quite another to be down there in the mud and mire with the writhing and hopeless and saying, "Yes, I know how much you ache; I know how impossible it seems; I was there. But hang on, man; Jesus will be here any minute to help. He did it for me and I know He'll do it for you."

Just as Jesus came down from heaven to participate in our sufferings, it shouldn't come as too big a surprise that we are called to participate in the sufferings of others.

## TO MAKE US COMPLETE, LACKING NOTHING

This is the final and perhaps most important reason we suffer.

> Consider it pure joy, my brothers, whenever you face trials of many kinds, because you know that the testing of your faith develops perseverance. Perseverance must finish its work so that you may be mature and complete, not lacking anything.
>
> James 1:2-4

I doubt there's a one of us who feels totally "complete" and "not lacking anything." And for good reason—we're not. Sin's taken quite a toll in our lives. I guess you could say that, one way or another, we're all walking around with crippled souls. But God, the great therapist, loves us too much to let us hobble around forever. He works with us, He forces us to take that extra step, to run that extra lap, to do that extra pull-up—no matter how painful it may seem.

Why? Because of His love. Because, like a dedicated coach who pushes us to the limit to strengthen us and make us winners, God will use our sufferings as a training tool to make us whole, to turn us into everything we can possibly be—to make us "mature and complete, not lacking anything."

Like a good coach, He wants what's best for us, even though we may not see it at the moment. Without the pain there would be no gain.

The disciple Peter puts it another way:

So be truly glad! There is wonderful joy ahead, even though the going is rough for a while down here. These trials are only to test your faith, to see whether or not it is strong and pure. It is being tested as fire tests gold and purifies it—and your faith is more precious to God than mere gold; so if your faith remains strong after being tried in the test tube of fiery trials, it will bring you much praise and glory and honor on the day of His return.

1 Peter 1:6-7 (TLB)

You see, in the old days when they used to smelt and purify gold, they would heat it up until the impurities in the ore surfaced. Then they'd scrape the worthless stuff off and heat up the remaining gold again . . . then again . . . and again—each time making the metal purer and purer.

And how did the refiner know when to stop? When he was able to look into the ore and see a perfect reflection of himself.

That's what God wants.

For from the very beginning God decided that those who came to Him . . . should become like His Son.

Romans 8:29 (TLB)

Jesus is the perfect example of being a whole, complete human being. He is the perfect example of being "mature and complete, not lacking anything." And, for our own happiness, that's what God wants for us. The purifying may not be pleasant, but it's definitely necessary.

## ▶ THE REAL QUESTION IS "HOW," NOT "WHY"

Although some pain was invented by God to protect us (like the pain from touching a hot stove), most of it has been invented or brought on by ourselves when we introduced sin into the world.

Yet, because "in all things God works together for the good of those who love Him" (Romans 8:28), He will take this terrible, hellish invention of ours and, if we love Him, somehow use it for our good. We may not see it right away. In fact we may never see it. God never did tell Job why (although before Job's life was over God gave him nearly double of everything the devil had destroyed).

But that shouldn't matter. Our question shouldn't be "Why?" it should be "How?" *How* can I use this to become everything You want me to be? *How* can I use this to draw closer to You? *How* can I use this to serve others better?

There is a world of difference between these two words. "Why?" is questioning, fighting, and doubting. "How?" is accepting whatever God has in mind and moving on to all that He wants us to be. Asking "How?" instead of "Why?" isn't easy. But it's always best.

Oh, one last thing. Remember all that emotional pain I went through just out of high school? Well, as a *direct* result of all that hurt, I gave up the 20 percent of my life that I was holding back from the Lord. And because of that commitment, I changed my major in college, married a wonderful wife, and travel all over the world writing and directing films—experiencing some pretty incredible adventures that I would never have even dreamed possible.

All of this because He loved me enough to allow me to suffer.

And all of this because I eventually stopped asking "Why?" and started asking "How?"

# DOPE AND BOOZE

▶ You don't have to be a nuclear scientist these days to figure out that doing drugs isn't so smart. The media, educators, and just about everybody else is jumping on the bandwagon, saying that if you play with drugs you'll get burned. And since God wants to give us "an abundant life," it's a safe guess that He's not too thrilled about us stir-frying ourselves either.

*But does the Bible say we can't do drugs?*

Not specifically. But neither does it say we shouldn't play with hand grenades or race down the freeway in the wrong direction.

Grass, crack, uppers, downers, PCP, and the rest weren't real hot items in the Bible days. But the one mind-altering chemical that was available at that time did manage to get some pretty bad press.

Wine is a mocker, strong drink a brawler, and whoever is intoxicated by it is not wise.

Proverbs 20:1 (NASB)

In the end it [alcohol] bites like a snake and poisons like a viper.

Proverbs 23:32

The acts of the sinful nature are obvious: sexual immorality . . . witchcraft; hatred . . . jealousy, fits of rage, selfish ambition, dissensions . . . envy, *drunkenness*, orgies and the like. *I warn you, as I did before, that those who live like this will not inherit the kingdom of God.*

Galatians 5:19-21
(italics added)

*Why? Why is God so down on relaxing and having a good time?*

That's not the case. Remember, He's on our side. He's not on some anti-fun campaign. He's not some pious killjoy waiting to stamp out the slightest resemblance to good times. On the contrary, He wants us to enjoy life, to enjoy it to the fullest, to be "mature and complete, not lacking anything" (James 1:4).

He just doesn't like it when we settle for some second-rate counterfeit, when we insist on playing with something that will burn and destroy us. And in the case of dope and booze, it's a three-way burn—physical, emotional, and spiritual.

## ▶ PHYSICAL BURN

Every drug, from alcohol to acid, is designed to short-circuit the body. That's what causes the buzz. One way or another, the chemical forces the body to start malfunctioning. And in each and every case, that malfunctioning, that poisoning, is going to take its toll—either in the form of addiction (physical or mental) or the destruction of healthy organs such as the heart, liver, nervous system, and brain.

But that's only for starters.

There isn't a drug out there that hasn't been cut with something by the time it gets to us. If we're smoking pot we'll probably also be smoking fertilizer. Doing mescaline? Count on a bad batch of LSD with some PCP thrown in for good measure. The list goes on. . . .

And forget quality control. We're not talking your sparkling-clean pharmaceutical lab here. We're talking grungy basements or bathrooms. We're talking dealers looking out for the dollars, not for your health.

Since there is no quality control, you may be doing one drug for months and then, without knowing it, you're doing the same amount but from a batch five times stronger. And then, without knowing it, you get to ride in an ambulance—or a hearse.

And finally, in the physical department, there are dangers of our own actions while under the influence. Actions such as:

• the high rate of suicides from the depression that follows;

- the fact that one out of every five accidents is drug/alcohol related—which, by the way, makes substance abuse the *number one killer of teenagers*;
- the frightening number of murders and self-mutilations—like the girl who ate her fingers while doing angel dust.

## ▶ EMOTIONAL BURN

But the physical dangers of substance abuse are small change compared to what happens emotionally.

If you're a teenager, right now you're going through some of the most important years of your life. This is the time that you figure out who you are, what you believe, where you're going, and how you're going to get there. (All this and zits too!)

Talk about pressure.

Unfortunately, studies show that one of the main reasons teens do drugs is to avoid that pressure. Instead of choosing to make the decisions that will shape the rest of their lives, instead of allowing the pressures to strengthen and refine them into adults, they take the easy way out—they escape.

And as a result of that escape they become *stunted*. God's plans to mature them, to make them "whole and complete," are foiled. They may have adult bodies, but there will be portions of their minds and emotions that are years behind—portions that, for all intents and purposes, are retarded.

DOPE AND BOOZE   **79**

## ▶ SPIRITUAL BURN

Another reason people turn to drugs is to fill up that emptiness, that void they feel inside. Some people describe it as a gnawing hunger; others refer to it as a constant thirst that never quite goes away.

Jesus understood this emptiness and did a lot of talking about it. Not only did He talk about it, but He showed us the only real cure for emptiness—Himself:

> I am the bread of life. He who comes to Me will never go hungry, and he who believes in Me will never be thirsty.
>
> John 6:35

The problem is that a lot of people won't turn to that cure. Or if they do, they'll only do it superficially, refusing to allow their relationship with Jesus to become intense enough to really help.

So instead of relying on the real thing and allowing Jesus to fill the emptiness, they keep turning to the quick fix. As they keep using the counterfeit, their spirit—which is what's really crying out to be fed and watered—slowly starves and withers.

Almost before they know it, their spirit becomes just as stunted and retarded as their emotions.

I've never talked to any regular user who didn't agree that he or she has been robbed—physically, emotionally, and spiritually.

## ▶ WEEKEND WARRIOR

*But what about a little partying—or just a little experimentation to find out what all the fuss is about?*

There is not a single addict or alcoholic in the world who didn't start off with this thinking.

No one imagines he's going to be emotionally or physically dependent. Every one of us is positive that we're different, that we're stronger, that we can beat it. There isn't a one of our nation's 10 million alcoholics or 8 million regular cocaine users that thought that first drink or line would be a problem.

And yet, did you know that studies prove that one out of every five who try cocaine for the first time become dependent upon the drug? One out of five!

And according to the National Institute on Alcohol Abuse and Alcoholism, it is nearly that same percentage of teenagers across America (one out of five) that have become problem drinkers.

One out of five! Those are terrible odds. A friend of mine compared it to playing Russian roulette. But he's wrong. The chance of losing in Russian roulette is *lower* (one out of six) than the chance of becoming a druggie or alcoholic!

## ▶ MARIJUANA

Since we usually consider this the "safe" drug, I thought I'd include a little information found in Jay Strack's book *Drugs and Drinking*, published by Thomas Nelson Publishers:

The National Institute on Drug Abuse has sponsored more than one thousand experimental projects concerning marijuana. Prominent among the findings in these documents are that marijuana use impairs memory, learning and speech . . . has negative effects in terms of heart rate and lung capacity, introduces cancer-causing hydrocarbons into the lungs, may affect the reproductive functions, leads to psychological problems in youthful users, induces feelings of paranoia and can lead to panic anxiety reactions. Regular use—even once or twice a week—means the user is never entirely free of the drug. (p. 38)

### ▶ ALCOHOL

I know we've already mentioned the high percentage of teenagers that can't control their drinking. But since we're quoting from Jay Strack, I thought I'd throw in some more info on the subject:

Alcoholism is America's third largest health problem, following heart disease and cancer.

It affects ten million people, costs sixty billion dollars, and is implicated in two hundred thousand deaths annually. Alcohol is involved in 50 percent of deaths by motor vehicle and fire, 67 percent of murders, and 33 percent of suicides.

It contributes to morbidity in certain malignancies and to many diseases of the endocrine, cardiovascular, gastrointestinal, and nervous systems. (p. 41)

The suicide rate of alcoholics has been found to be six to twenty times higher than that of the general population. (p. 44)

With this damaging evidence, if alcohol were to be presented for legalization as a drug today, it surely would not be accepted. (p. 46)

Drugs and booze may be fun. But everyone from researchers to educators to regular users to God says that the good times are *not* worth the price of admission.

If you aren't doing drugs, don't.

If you are, stop.

## ▶ WHAT IF I CAN'T STOP?

The trouble with most people dependent on alcohol or drugs is that they don't know they have a problem. They figure they can stop anytime they want (and probably do stop—over and over and over again). But if you already know you have a problem, you're halfway home.

If you want to quit or know someone who does, here are five basic steps. If alcohol or drugs are *not* a problem in your life, please read these steps anyway. With the percentages as high as they are, you're bound to run into someone someday who will be looking for a way out.

## 1. BE HONEST

Do you really want to be free? Do you really want out? This may sound strange, but a lot of people who say they want to stop really don't. Oh, maybe part of them does, but the greater part just loves the good times too much.

Fortunately, this usually doesn't last too long. Eventually they're able to see the toll their dependency is starting to take. Eventually, like everyone else, they realize they have to get out.

## 2. TURN TO THE HEALER

Slowly tapering off is not the answer. No amount of self-will can cure. And drug rehab programs? According to U.S. government research, the best drug programs in the country have cure rates of only 3 to 10 percent. So what can be done?

Give up. Admit defeat—*total defeat*. Ask God to come in and take complete charge. Don't just give Him permission to come into a couple areas; give Him the whole house—access to every room, every hidden closet. Give Him permission to set you *completely* free. That's what He had in mind when He promised:

> He [the Father] has sent Me [Jesus] to
> proclaim freedom for the prisoners.
> Luke 4:18

So if the Son sets you free, you will be
free indeed.

John 8:36

I mentioned that most drug programs have a
cure rate of only 3 to 10 percent. That's not quite
true. Three to 10 percent is the cure rate for
most "secular" programs. But sold-out Christian
programs like Teen Challenge have an 86 percent
*permanent* cure rate. Eighty-six percent!

Because of that impressive rate, the U.S. government figured they'd better get in there and
find out what was happening. After months of
investigating the Teen Challenge program, they
could come up with only one significant difference. Its official name? "The Jesus factor."

### 3. FILL THE HOLE
Remember how we talked about drugs being used
as a substitute to fill the hole in our hearts that
was originally designed for Jesus? Well, without
drugs, that hole will still be there. So keep filling
it up with the Real Thing. Begin developing a
*close* friendship with Jesus, begin reading His
Word, begin praying.

### 4. FILL THE TIME
Keep busy! Now that you're regaining control of
your life, ask yourself what you want to do. What
were your ambitions before you got sidetracked?
Set some realistic goals for yourself, then set out
to accomplish them!

Just as you need to fill up your heart with

Jesus instead of drugs, you need to fill up your new spare time with *doing* instead of dreaming. I can't stress this enough. The times of becoming a couch potato are history. It's time to get back on the track. Because if you're not stepping out in a new direction, there's a strong possibility you'll be sucked back into the old.

## 5. LIVE THE NEW LIFE
Again quoting from Jay Strack:

> All your plans must start with God. Make Him your partner. Give God first chance to use your life. It may be He will want you to help other addicts when you are fully cured.
>
> You can never be around your old neighborhood or your old friends. Stay away from your old life as if it were hell itself. Stay away from your old hangouts instead of testing yourself to see if you are cured—that would be tempting God. Find new friends and brothers who are clean. (p. 194–195)

Lots of do's and don'ts here, I know. But sometimes when you drive off the road it takes a little effort to get back on.

The good news is, it's possible. It may not be easy, but it is possible.

> I can do *everything* through Him who gives me strength.
> Philippians 4:13 (italics added)

In all these things we are more than conquerors through Him who loved us.

Romans 8:37

# IS THERE A HEAVEN?

▶ Everyone likes to believe there's a heaven. You know, the place where all us good folk go and finally get our goodies—that big awards assembly in the sky.

But what is heaven really like? And to be more honest, how do we know it really exists? Could we just be fooling ourselves with a little wishful thinking? Where's the proof?

Good questions. Let's see if there are some answers.

## ▶ JESUS BELIEVED

For starters, Jesus believed there is a heaven.

> Rejoice and be glad, because great is
> your reward in heaven.
>
> Matthew 5:12

In fact, He made it pretty clear that He considered heaven home base:

> Father, glorify Me in Your presence
> with the glory I had with You before
> the world began.
>
> John 17:5

He also made it pretty clear that that's where He was going:

> In my Father's house are many rooms;
> if it were not so, I would have told you.
> I am going there to prepare a place for
> you. And if I go and prepare a place for
> you, I will come back and take you to
> be with Me that you also may be where
> I am.
>
> John 14:2-3

And finally, He wasted no words telling us that the only way for us to get there is *through* Him:

> I am the way and the truth and the
> life. No one comes to the Father except
> through Me.
>
> John 14:6

So as far as Jesus was concerned, there was definitely a heaven, a place where people who put their trust in Him would go.

## ▶ WHAT'S IT LIKE?

In the book of Revelation, the Apostle John recounts his quick tour of the place. This is *some* of what he saw:

In a vision he took me to a towering mountain peak and from there I watched that wondrous city, the holy Jerusalem, descending out of the skies from God. It was filled with the glory of God, and flashed and glowed like a precious gem, crystal clear like jasper.

When he [the angel tour guide] measured it, he found it was a square as wide as it was long; in fact it was in the form of a cube, for its height was exactly the same as its other dimensions—1,500 miles each way.

The city itself was pure, transparent gold like glass! The wall was made of jasper, and was built on twelve layers of foundation stones, inlaid with gems.

Nothing evil will be permitted in it—no one immoral or dishonest—but only those whose names are written in the Lamb's Book of Life.

And He pointed out to me a river of pure Water of Life, clear as crystal, flowing from the throne of God and the Lamb, coursing down the center of the main street.

Revelation 21:10-11, 16, 18-19, 27;
22:1-2 (TLB)

And this is only *part* of what He saw.

But you know, descriptions of heaven aren't just in the Bible (though that should be enough). Reliable witnesses who, through modern medicine, have died and been brought back to life again also believe they've seen this "celestial city." And although we have to be careful never to take any personal account as seriously as we do the Holy Word of God, it's interesting that many people, some who haven't read the Bible, have given exactly the same description.

Here are just a few of numerous eyewitness accounts.

> And then I saw, infinitely far off, far too distant to be visible with any kind of sight I knew of . . . a city. A glowing . . . city, bright enough to be seen over all the unimaginable distance between. The lightness seemed to shine from the very walls and streets of this place, and from beings which I could now discern moving about within it. In fact, the city and everything in it seemed to be made of light. *(Return from Tomorrow,* George G. Ritchie with Elizabeth Sherrill, Spire Books, p. 72)

> I noticed I was crossing over a beautiful city below, as I followed the river like a soaring bird. The streets seemed to be made of shining gold and were wonderfully beautiful. I can't describe it. I descended into one of the streets and people were all around me—happy people who were glad to see me! They seemed to be in shining clothes with a sort of glow. *(Beyond Death's Door,*

Maurice Rawlings, M.D., Bantam Books, p. 76)

As I approached him I felt a great reverence and I asked him, "Are you Jesus?"

He said, "No, you will find Jesus and your loved ones beyond that door." After he looked in his book he said, "You may go on through."

And then I walked through the door, and saw on the other side this beautiful, brilliantly lit city. . . . It was all made of gold or something metal with domes and steeples in beautiful array, and the streets were shining. . . . There were many people all dressed in glowing white robes with radiant faces. They looked beautiful. (*Beyond Death's Door,* p. 80)

But there's another interesting similarity between what John saw and what some of those who feel they've seen heaven can recall. Remember 1 Timothy 6:15-16, where God is described as so holy that He lives in this "unapproachable light"? In nearly every account there's mention of an incredibly bright being—whose very presence seems to light the city—somebody whom everyone seems to be worshiping.

His face was like the sun shining in all its brilliance.

Revelation 1:16

I saw that it was not light but a Man
. . . a man made out of light, though
this seemed no more possible to my
mind than the incredible intensity of
the brightness that made up His form.
*(Return from Tomorrow,* pp. 48–49)

No temple could be seen in the city,
for the Lord God Almighty and the
Lamb [Jesus] are worshiped in it everywhere. And the city has no need of sun
or moon to light it, for the glory of
God and the Lamb illuminate it.
Revelation 21:22-23 (TLB)

## ▶ WHAT DOES IT FEEL LIKE?

Most people describe heaven or their experience
of standing in front of Jesus as an intense love
and breathtaking awe. It's as if all of the worries
and troubles of the world suddenly mean nothing
when compared to what they see. The only thing
that matters is the love and awesome power they
experience radiating from Jesus Christ.

The instant I perceived Him, a command formed itself in my mind. "Stand
up!" The words came from inside me,
yet they had an authority my mere
thoughts had never had. I got to my
feet, and as I did came the stupendous
certainty: "You are in the presence of
*the* Son of God."

Again, the concept seemed to form
itself inside me, but not as thought or

speculation. It was a kind of knowing, immediate and complete. . . . If this was *the* Son of God, then His name was Jesus. But . . . this was not the Jesus of my Sunday School books. That Jesus was gentle, kind, understanding—and probably a little bit of a weakling. This Person was power itself, older than time and yet more modern than anyone I had ever met.

Above all, with that same mysterious inner certainty, I knew that this Man loved me. Far more even than the power, what emanated from this Presence was unconditional love. An astonishing love. A love beyond my wildest imagining. This love knew every unlovable thing about me—the quarrels with my stepmother, my explosive temper, the sex thoughts I could never control, every mean, selfish thought and action since the day I was born— and accepted and loved me just the same. *(Return from Tomorrow,* p. 49)

Billy Graham, in his book on dying, describes what he believes heaven to "feel" like:

Have you ever watched young couples in love communicate without words? Have you been in love yourself? People deeply in love find absolute bliss in each other's presence and wish their moments together would go on forever. If those moments could be frozen, with no sense of passing time, would that be "heaven" for them? . . .

I suspect those feelings are a small indication of what it would be like, frozen in time and loving God, enjoying Him, forever. (*Facing Death and the Life After,* Word Books, p. 223)

These are great descriptions. But remember, they are only personal experiences or opinions. And both can sometimes be wrong. The real proof lies in what the Bible teaches:

Now the dwelling of God is with men, and He will live with them. They will be His people, and God Himself will be with them and be their God. He will wipe every tear from their eyes. There will be no more death or mourning or crying or pain.

Revelation 21:3-4

Sounds pretty good to me!

The point is, if Jesus left earth to prepare a place for us in heaven, chances are it must be pretty awesome.

Or, as the Bible puts it:

No eye has seen, no ear has heard, no mind has conceived what God has prepared for those who love Him.

1 Corinthians 2:9

## ▶ HOW DO WE GET THERE?

No discussion of heaven would be complete without mentioning how we get there. Despite the rumors, we don't get there through good works, or through being super religious, or even by going to church every Sunday.

As Jesus said, there's one way and one way only—through Him.

> For God so loved the world that He gave His one and only Son, that whoever believes in Him shall not perish but have eternal life. For God did not send His Son into the world to condemn the world, but to save the world through Him.
>
> John 3:16-17

# IS HELL FOR REAL?

▶ *You keep saying, "God is love, God is love."*
*So tell me, how could this God of love send any-*
*body to some great, eternal barbeque pit?*

We've all heard this question a dozen times
before (and probably thought it just as often).
Let's face it, for many of us hell is an embarrassing subject—definitely uncool (in more ways
than one). I mean, unless someone is telling
somebody to go there, no one really wants to
bring up the subject.

But, as we've said before, God's pretty secure
with who He is and isn't too concerned about
fitting into what's cool and what's not. He's managed to run the universe without our help and
opinions this long; chances are He'll continue to
do so for a while longer. And, whether we like it
or not, there's most definitely a hell.

I tell you, My friends, do not be afraid of those who kill the body and after that can do no more. But I will show you whom you should fear: Fear Him who, after the killing of the body, has power to throw you into hell. Yes, I tell you, fear Him.

Luke 12:4-5

The Son of Man will send out His angels, and they will weed out of His kingdom everything that causes sin and all who do evil. They will throw them into the fiery furnace, where there will be weeping and gnashing of teeth.

Matthew 13:41-42

It is better for you to lose one part of your body than for your whole body to be thrown into hell.

Matthew 5:29

You snakes! You brood of vipers! How will you escape being condemned to hell?

Matthew 23:33

Yes, by these verses (and others), it's a safe guess that God wants us to take this place called hell pretty seriously.

## ▶ WHAT'S IT LIKE?

First of all, anybody that winds up calling it home will be totally cut off from God. His holiness, His glory, and most important His love—all the things that we've seen in the last chapter which make heaven such a great place—will be completely gone.

> They will be punished with everlasting destruction and shut out from the presence of the Lord and from the majesty of His power.
>
> 2 Thessalonians 1:9

Bad news. And with the absence of God comes the absence of His light and the absence of His love, making it a place of "darkness, where there will be weeping and gnashing of teeth" (Matthew 22:13).

Sounds harsh, I know. But if people keep telling God to butt out of their lives, that they want nothing to do with Him, He's eventually going to let them have their way—forever.

## ▶ PHYSICAL DESCRIPTIONS

Just as John got a tour of heaven when he was inspired to write the Book of Revelation, he also got a glimpse of hell.

> When he opened the Abyss, smoke rose from it like the smoke from a gigantic furnace. The sun and sky were darkened by the smoke from the Abyss.
>
> Revelation 9:2

> The two of them were thrown alive into the fiery lake of burning sulfur.
>
> Revelation 19:20

If anyone's name was not found written in the book of life, he was thrown into the lake of fire.

> Revelation 20:15

Then there's Jesus' parable about the suffering poor man and the greedy rich man:

The time came when the beggar died and the angels carried him to Abraham's side [heaven]. The rich man also died and was buried. In hell, where he was in torment, he looked up and saw Abraham far away, with Lazarus by his side. So he called to him, "Father Abraham, have pity on me and send Lazarus to dip the tip of his finger in water and cool my tongue, because I am in agony in this fire."

But Abraham replied, "Son, remember that in your lifetime you received your good things, while Lazarus received bad things, but now he is comforted here and you are in agony. And besides all this, between us and you a great chasm has been fixed, so that those who want to go from here to you cannot, nor can anyone cross over from there to us.

> Luke 16:22-26

▶ *OTHER DESCRIPTIONS*
*But what about all these people who die and come back to life? They always talk about heav-*

*en; you never hear them talking about hell.*

Not true.

Dr. Maurice Rawlings, in his book *Beyond Death's Door,* tells of a patient whose heart stopped while undergoing tests in his office. Through heart massage the doctor was able to bring him back to life. But not for long. As the doctor kept working on him, trying to insert a pacemaker, the guy kept dying on him. And each time the patient regained consciousness he screamed, "I am in hell!"

Now heart massage can be a painfully brutal experience; many have even had their ribs broken in the process. But instead of pleading for the doctor to stop, as is normally the case, the patient begged him to continue. Of course the doctor was dumbfounded, but there was more.

> I noticed a genuinely alarmed look on his face. He had a terrified look *worse* than the expression seen in death! This patient had a grotesque grimace expressing sheer horror! His pupils were dilated, and he was perspiring and trembling—he looked as if his hair was "on end."
>
> Then still another strange thing happened. He said, "Don't you understand? I am in hell. Each time you quit I go back to hell! Don't let me go back to hell!" (p. 3)

After clinically dying a few more times, the patient began pleading with the doctor for some way to stay out of the place. And although the doctor didn't know much about prayer, he did know something about Jesus Christ. And together the two prayed for Christ to save the patient.

Well, the patient eventually recovered. But when Dr. Rawlings talked to him a few days later, the man didn't remember a thing.

"What hell? I don't recall any hell!"

Rawlings described in detail all that had happened, but the patient still could not recall a single one of the "unpleasant events." After giving it careful consideration, the doctor's final conclusion was this:

> Apparently the experiences were so frightening, so horrible, so painful that his conscious mind could not cope with them; and they were subsequently suppressed far into his subconscious. (p. 5)

This may be one reason so few people who have died and come back to life are able to recall being in hell.

But from the unlucky ones who can remember (and there are quite a few) come descriptions very close to the Bible's:

> I was standing some distance from this burning, turbulent, rolling mass of blue fire. As far as my eyes could see it was just the same. A lake of fire and brimstone. . . . There is no way to escape, no way out. You don't even try to

look for one. This is the prison out of which no one can escape except by Divine intervention. (Thomas Welch, *Oregon's Amazing Miracle* [Dallas: Christ for the Nations, Inc., 1976], p. 8, as quoted by *Beyond Death's Door*, p. 87)

▶ *AWAITING JUDGMENT?*
*But what about those who deny Christ and still claim they were in heaven—you know, saying they were surrounded by smiling relatives or greeted by some "loving light" at the end of a tunnel?*

A good question.

But from the experiences I've read and researched, this is often just the first phase of death. Others who have gone further into the death experience talk about a wall or barrier they eventually come to and cannot cross over. Some talk about waiting in a holding area. If this is the case, then perhaps they really are in heaven, but just in a waiting room where they are received until it's their turn to be judged.

And if that's true, and their names are *not* in Jesus' "book of life," imagine how horrific it must be to be yanked away from all the love they're surrounded with and wind up in hell.

Again, keep in mind that these human experiences are not to be considered on the same level as the Scripture. But also keep in mind that both Jesus and the Bible speak quite seriously about this place of eternal punishment, and that anyone whose name is not written in the "Lamb's book of life" is heading there.

## ▶ WHY?
*If God is so loving, why would He want to send anyone there?*

First of all, God doesn't want to send anybody to hell.

> He is patient with you, not wanting anyone to perish, but everyone to come to repentance.
>
> 2 Peter 3:9

He wants so desperately for us to stay out of the place that He came down from heaven and suffered and died the most agonizing and humiliating death imaginable just to keep us from it. (Doesn't sound like anyone too interested in roasting people to me.)

You see, the problem is not with God; it's with us. As a race, we're the ones who told Him to get lost; we're the ones who told Him to take a hike back in the Garden of Eden. And even today when we sin as individuals we're saying exactly the same thing: "Leave me alone, God. I want to do it my way, not Yours."

Fortunately some of us eventually begin to realize our way is not so hot, and we want to come back to God. And for those who are serious, He has provided a way, an instantaneous way for us to get back into His presence: through the sacrifice Jesus Christ made for us on that cross.

The point is, we're the ones responsible for cutting God off; we're the ones responsible for this disease called sin. It's our fault, not His.

## ALL THIS TO SAY . . .

Hell is real. Very real.

And it's not too terribly hard to imagine. It is *complete and total separation* from God.

- Its *darkness* is the complete absence of *God's holiness*.
- Its *misery* is the complete absence of *God's love*.
- Its *torment* is the complete absence of *God's forgiveness*.

The Lord doesn't want anyone to experience that separation. In His intense love for us, God has provided the cure. And anyone, no matter who they are, no matter what they've done, can receive that cure and return to God's presence, no strings attached. All they have to do is ask.

But if they don't want to, if they keep refusing God and continue to insist on being separated from Him, He will let them have their way—for eternity.

# DEATH AND SUICIDE

▶ Death is a reality.

No matter how much we hate it or try to ignore it, it's still going to happen—to each of us. Count on it. As the playwright George Bernard Shaw put it, "The statistics on death are quite impressive. One out of one people die."

## ▶ WHY?

Dying is definitely not on my top-10 list of things to do. It separates, it destroys, it deprives. There is nothing harsher than ripping someone away from friends and loved ones, destroying all hopes and dreams, and depriving them of all that they could do and all that they could be.

*So why? Why, if there's a loving God, did He invent such a miserable thing? Why does He make us go through it?*

Unfortunately, just like suffering, death wasn't in God's original game plan. Death wasn't God's choice; it was ours.

> When Adam sinned, sin entered the entire human race. His sin spread death throughout all the world, so everything began to grow old and die, for all sinned.
>
> Romans 5:12 (TLB)

So death comes as a direct result of sin. But before we come down too hard on Adam, remember the Bible says we're all guilty, "for *all* sinned."

But for those of us who realize we've made a mistake—for those of us who want to start following God's plan—as always, He's provided a way out.

> Adam's *one* sin brought the penalty of death to many, while Christ freely takes away *many* sins and gives glorious life instead. The sin of this one man, Adam, caused *death to be king over all,* but all who will take God's gift of forgiveness and acquittal are *kings of life* because of this one man, Jesus Christ.
>
> Romans 5:16-17 (TLB)

That doesn't mean we can skip death like some class we're ditching. But for the Christian, instead of a time of fear and agony, death becomes more like graduation day: a time for moving onward to bigger and better things.

So what's it like? We've touched on this when we talked about heaven and hell. Here's a little more of what you can expect if you have turned your life over to Christ.

### ▶ IMMEDIATELY WITH JESUS

Contrary to what some teach we are not doomed to:

- floating around and haunting houses,
- making guest appearances at seances,
- coming back in different lives until we finally get it right,
- falling into a deep sleep until Jesus returns, or
- going to some holding pen (purgatory) until our sins are paid off.

Instead, as best as we can understand from the Scriptures, as soon as we die we go to be with Jesus. Billy Graham, in his book *Facing Death and the Life After,* explains it like this:

> The believer's passage to heaven is a direct route. As soon as we are dead, we will be with the Lord. Jesus told the repentant thief on the cross, "I tell you the truth, today you will be with me in paradise" (Luke 23:43). Paul declared, "I desire to depart and be with Christ" (Philippians 1:23). He also affirmed, "Therefore we are always confident and know that as long as we are at home in the body we are away from the Lord. We live by faith, not by sight. We are

confident, I say, and would prefer to be away from the body and at home with the Lord" (2 Corinthians 5:6-8). (p. 238)

## ▶ WILL WE RECOGNIZE EACH OTHER?

Lots of people who have clinically died and then come back to life talk about meeting friends and loved ones who have already died and who come out to greet them as part of some welcoming committee. But again, keep in mind these are only personal experiences; they are not Scripture.

There is, however, some scriptural indication that we'll recognize each other. Back in Luke 9 a couple heavyweight Old Testament heroes who hadn't been around for centuries dropped by for a little chat.

Seems Jesus was on a mountaintop with some of His disciples when suddenly Moses and Elijah appeared and started talking with Him about His upcoming death on the cross. It's doubtful these guys were wearing any name tags, but somehow, some way, the disciples immediately recognized who they were.

OK, so as soon as our physical body dies, our spirit goes to be with the Lord, and we'll probably all recognize each other. But it doesn't stop there. Eventually, when Jesus returns to earth, we'll go through another transformation. When Jesus returns from heaven to set up rule on earth, our old, decayed carcasses will be resurrected from the dead and changed into brand-new bodies.

## ▶ SUPERHUMAN BODIES

> When He comes back He will take
> these dying bodies of ours and change
> them into glorious bodies like His
> own.
>
> Philippians 3:21 (TLB)

A body "like His own." Not a bad deal, considering that with His resurrected body Jesus was in perfect health and was able to do things like walk through closed doors, suddenly appear to people, zip up to heaven. And we're not talking some sort of ghost or spirit here. He did all of these things with a physical body that could actually eat and that people could actually touch.

So if you think you got the short end of the stick with a crummy body now, rest assured it won't always be that way.

> Yes, they are weak, dying bodies now,
> but when we live again they will be full
> of strength. They are just human bod-
> ies at death, but when they come back
> to life they will be superhuman bodies.
>
> 1 Corinthians 15:43-44 (TLB)

## ▶ WHAT DO WE DO UP THERE?

*No offense, but if all we do in heaven is sit around playing harps and floating on clouds, that doesn't sound like my idea of paradise.*

Mine either.

The good news is the Bible never talks about harp plucking or cloud floating. What it does talk about is being able to really get into loving and praising and worshiping God and becoming like Jesus.

Oh, there's one more thing we'll be doing: helping Him rule the universe.

Find that a little hard to swallow? I did. At first it sounds a little farfetched. But it's right there in the Book:

> To him who overcomes, I will give the right to sit with Me on My throne, just as I overcame and sat down with My Father on His throne.
>
> Revelation 3:21

> The Spirit Himself testifies with our spirit that we are God's children. Now if we are children, then we are heirs—heirs of God and co-heirs with Christ, if indeed we share in His sufferings in order that we may also share in His glory.
>
> Romans 8:16-17

And finally:

> Do you not know that the saints [that's us] will judge the world? . . . Do you not know that we will judge angels?
>
> 1 Corinthians 6:2-3

Pretty impressive. To really worship Jesus, *and* to share in His glory, *and* to help Him rule the universe—well, that sounds like a program worth signing up for.

## ▶ SO WHAT?
*But what's all this got to do with me now, today?*

A good question. And the answer is simple: "Everything." Because how we live today is going to determine how we live after we die. Let me say that again. What we do now is going to have a direct effect on how we spend eternity.

First, there's the heaven-or-hell decision. Do we want to take the punishment for our sins and suffer in hell, or do we want Jesus to take that punishment so we can live in heaven? A stupid question, I know. Unfortunately, too many people are coming up with an even more stupid answer.

But what about those of us who've made the right decision and are heading to heaven? Does how we live now really make any difference on how we live then? Heaven is heaven, right?

Yes and no. We'll all be there, true—*but* each of us will be *judged* and *rewarded* by how we served God down here.

> For we will all stand before God's judgment seat. . . . Each of us will give an account of himself to God.
>
> Romans 14:10, 12

> So we make it our goal to please Him, whether we are at home in the body or away from it. For we must all appear before the judgment seat of Christ, that each one may receive what is due him for the things done while in the body, whether good or bad.
>
> 2 Corinthians 5:9-10

You see, if we've asked Jesus to take the rap for our wrongdoings and to become our Lord but we spend all our time down here pursuing selfish pleasures and goals or building our lives with things that don't really count . . . well, according to the Bible, we may be in for a little disappointment:

> No one can ever lay any other real foundation than that one we already have—Jesus Christ. But there are various kinds of materials that can be used to build on that foundation. Some use gold and silver and jewels; and some build with sticks, and hay, or even straw! There is going to come a time of testing at Christ's Judgment Day to see what kind of material each builder has used. Everyone's work will be put through the fire so that all can see whether or not it keeps its value, and what was really accomplished. Then every workman who has built on the foundation with the right materials, and whose work still stands, will get his pay. But if the house he has built burns up, he will have a great loss. He himself will be saved, but like a man escaping through a wall of flames.
> 1 Corinthians 3:11-15 (TLB)

In other words, if you build your life with eternal things (love and service to God and fellow folks), you'll have phenomenal rewards in heaven.

If you build your life with worthless stuff (money, fame, and selfish desires), you'll make it to heaven OK if you're a Christian, but you won't have anything to show for your life but ashes.

## ▶ SUICIDE

There is nothing more tragic than the act of someone taking and destroying his or her own life, especially when that person is young with an entire future ahead.

And yet suicide is the number two killer of teens in America. This year alone, two *million* teenagers will attempt suicide. *TWO MILLION!* That's nearly 5,500 young people a day!

Why? What's going on? And more important, what can we do to help?

### LIFE IN THE PRESSURE COOKER

There is no other time of life where you'll be going through so many changes and have to make so many decisions as during your teen years. In those few short years from age 13 to 19 you're suddenly thrust out of cozy childhood and forced to make major choices about:
- who you are,
- what you believe,
- how you'll live your life,
- what you'll do with your life,
- what your standards are.

And if that's not enough there's:
- school,
- peer pressure,
- sexual pressure,

- social pressure,
- parent pressure,
- loneliness,
- self-acceptance,
- radical chemical changes,
- first loves,
- no loves,
- that ever-transforming body.

## ROLLER-COASTER EMOTIONS

There is no other time in your life that you will experience such exhilarating highs—and such devastating lows. You're in the midst of a thousand first-time experiences, and first-time experiences are always the best—and the worst. It's a roller-coaster ride full of Death Valleys and Mount Everests. As you get older, these peaks and valleys start to level out because you have other experiences to compare them with. But for now they can be tough.

When older adults hit long-term bad situations, they know from experience that they won't last forever. But when young people enter deep, long-term heartache or depression, they can grow terribly hopeless—they have no past experience to prove to them that things will eventually get better. So they take the ultimate escape.

But what's so sad is that if they'd have waited, or if they would have gotten help, the pain and hopelessness would have eventually disappeared. Emotional wounds are just like physical wounds. It may take time, it may take outside help, but if you're willing to take that time and get that help, they will *always* heal. *ALWAYS*.

## ▶ WHAT CAN I DO?

If you're reading this now and think life isn't worth the hassle, that there's too much pressure, or that you're in a pit too deep for anyone to help, please, *please* talk to somebody. There are people who have been where you are, people who have seen nothing but utter blackness and hopelessness. And yet, by talking to someone, they've managed to make it through those troubled waters.

You see, Jesus wasn't fooling when he called Satan a "thief" who wants to "steal and kill and destroy." Don't let the little creep have his way. Get help. Find somebody you can trust, somebody you can talk freely to, somebody who knows how to listen. Maybe a pastor, a youth worker, a counselor at school, or just a *mature* friend in Christ.

You do not need to fight this battle on your own. Christ loved you enough to die for you. Give Him a chance to help. He made you special and unique, and He has a lifetime of hopes and plans for you. Please don't short-circuit Him; please don't cut Him off before He really gets you started.

Just as He said Satan came to kill and destroy, He promised that He (Jesus) came so "that they [you] might have life, and have it abundantly" (John 10:10, NASB).

You may not see it yet, but that's His plan. Just give Him a chance to get it in full operation.

## IF YOU KNOW SOMEONE

If someone you know is talking about suicide, be his or her friend. Don't try to preach or to be some sort of cheerleader. Just listen and ache and cry with your friend. That's part of what Jesus did with His suffering friends, and that's some of the best help any of us can offer.

If the situation arises, tactfully offer words of hope. Try to help your friend see the fuller picture—that the pain will go away and that God's got a lifetime of better things in store. And above all, let someone you both trust, like a counselor or pastor, know as soon as possible.

## CAN'T SUICIDE MAKE SITUATIONS BETTER?

That's usually what the person who attempts it thinks. But here's what John Q. Baucom, in his book *Fatal Choice, the Teenage Suicide Crisis,* says:

> Even at their best, suicide attempts are devastating to the family and the victim. Successful suicides are even more damaging. The emotional trauma experienced by family and friends ranges from extreme guilt to denial, rage, and profound anguish. People blame themselves for not noticing. Eventually they even blame each other as the reality becomes more confusing. It is quite common for families of both unsuccessful and successful suicide attempts to eventually experience depression

themselves and occasionally additional attempts.

Many people who attempt suicide do so under the misconception that it will "make things better." In my professional experience *I am aware of no cases where that has been true."* (Moody Press, p. 95, italics added)

## WILL SOMEONE WHO'S COMMITTED SUICIDE GO TO HELL?

No one can say for sure, but I strongly doubt it. Not if he or she has really made Jesus Lord. The whole reason Jesus came was to forgive us of our sins, no matter how terrible they may be. And suicide, no matter how rebellious towards God's plans or how selfish and self-centered, is not a sin that God is unable to forgive. I personally believe He can and will forgive anyone who has seriously accepted Jesus and has asked Him to forgive his sins.

> For I am convinced that neither death nor life, neither angels nor demons, neither the present nor the future, nor any powers, neither height nor depth, nor anything else in all creation, will be able to separate us from the love of God that is in Christ Jesus our Lord.
>                                     Romans 8:38

## ALL THIS TO SAY . . .

Death is a horrible, destructive thing that we human-types have brought upon ourselves through sin. But, as always, God has taken something horrific and, for those who follow Him, has turned it around into a type of blessing—a graduation into a life full of His presence.

> Death has been swallowed up in victory. Where, O death, is your victory? Where, O death, is your sting? . . . Thanks be to God! He gives us the victory through our Lord Jesus Christ.
>
> 1 Corinthians 15:54-55, 57

# WHAT'S ALL THIS NEW AGE STUFF?

▶ The last thing in the world I want to do is stand on some street corner and start screaming that something's from the devil. Talk about closed-minded. But I don't know what else to say about this subject. It seems to be everywhere and millions of people (including naive Christians) are being sucked into it every year. So . . . *"LOOK OUT, IT'S FROM THE DEVIL!"* There, thanks for letting me get it off my chest. Now let's see what "it" is.

## ▶ A NONRELIGION RELIGION

Although the New Age movement involves religious thinking, it is not an official religion with official headquarters, official spokespersons, or official leaders. It's more of a way of thinking than a religion. There are no fancy fireworks, fanfares, or telethons. Instead, the New Age movement spreads like water; it keeps a low profile while managing to seep, almost unnoticed, into our society—from the Star Wars film sagas to Saturday morning cartoon magic and mysticism to some relaxation techniques used in schools—the list goes on.

On the surface most New Age thinking sounds really great. Often the goal seems to be to get us more in tune with God and to help us become all that He designed us to be. What could be better or more spiritual? In addition, New Age thinking often uses Christian phrases, biblical concepts, and even parts of the Bible. And most of the New Agers will readily admit that Jesus Christ is God's son.

*So what's the problem?*

The problem is that it's a con job. Not the people, mind you. They're usually good, sincere folk. But they've bought into a false bill of goods. It's true they are drawing closer to a supernatural force all right—the only problem is, it's the *wrong* one.

Once you get past all the positive thinking, fancy phrases, and Christian-sounding concepts, you eventually discover something much darker. You discover that New Age thinking can be boiled down to one thing: it is simply a hodgepodge of demonic practices from the Eastern religions with just enough Christianity thrown in so we'll swallow the bait. Unfortunately it isn't until the bait goes down that people discover there's a hook buried inside.

## SOME TIP-OFFS

Usually New Age thinking will involve some sort of belief or practice in:

- reincarnation,
- astrology,
- mystical and out-of-body experiences,
- channeling (spirits speaking through a person),
- crystal power,
- yoga,
- meditation,
- imaginary guides,
- some forms of positive thinking,
- certain relaxation techniques,
- altered states of consciousness,
- self-improvement programs.

## IS IT REALLY SO WRONG?

*Come on, not all of that stuff is so bad. A Christian can believe in some of it.*

Let's take a closer look at a few of the major beliefs and practices, then compare them to what the Bible says.

## ▶ *REINCARNATION*

I've just returned from a heartbreaking trip to Asia, where I saw incredible indifference toward human suffering. Children and adults were begging, dying, starving, rotting away with leprosy in the streets—and no one seemed to care. And the countries where the lack of concern was the worst were the countries who believed in reincarnation the most.

Why?

Reincarnation basically states that the life you live today is a direct result of the way you lived a past life. If you were a good guy in the past life, things are going to go better for you this time around. If you were a jerk the last time, you'll pay for it by coming back as a bottom-of-the-heap person.

So if I believe that today's suffering people are just paying for their past sins, why should I interfere with "God's punishment" by trying to make their lives easier? In fact it would be better for me *not* to help the poor and suffering so they'll hurry up and die and graduate to a higher lifestyle the next time around.

Now picture an entire society living under that type of thinking for centuries and you can start to understand why they have such intense poverty and disrespect for human life.

And yet, with such clear-cut examples of what reincarnation thinking does to society, today one out of three American college students believes in it. *One out of three.* And sadly, many of them are Christian—even though belief in reincarnation is in *direct opposition to the Bible*.

Reincarnation teaches that we keep dying and coming back to life. The Bible says:

> Man is destined to die *once,* and after
> that to face judgment.
> > Hebrews 9:27 (italics added)

Reincarnation goes against the very basis of Christianity. In the first *Hot Topics, Tough Questions,* we explained it this way:

Reincarnation teaches that the only way we can get rid of our sin is to go through several different lifetimes until we finally work it out. Jesus, on the other hand, says that He came to pay the entire price of our sins. In fact, that was the whole purpose of His dying on the cross—to pay for our sins. If we believed in reincarnation, we'd believe that we can eventually work our way into heaven and don't need Jesus Christ. Our salvation would lie in what we could do, not in what Christ has already done. The entire theme of the New Testament is that man can *never* be saved through his efforts— that he can *only* be saved by his faith in Jesus Christ (Ephesians 2:8-9).

Now there's one other minor problem. . . .

What about all these people who are supposedly taken back into their past lives through hypnosis? How do they know facts and foreign languages that they've never heard before if they did not live back then? Again, some of this can be fraud and some just an overactive subconscious. But for the legitimate experiences there can only be one answer.

Robert A. Morey puts it best: "A hypnotic trance is the exact mental state which *mediums* and *witches* have been self-inducing for centuries in order to open themselves up to spirit or demonic control. Hypnotic regression to a 'past life' can easily be an occult experience."

He continues with what I consider the biggest red flag about this practice:

"Here lies the ultimate explanation for those 'unexplainable' recall cases. In every situation where a person recalled a 'past life,' and this life was researched and proven factual in even intimate details, and not fraudulent, *the person was involved in occult practices.* Supernatural knowledge was gained by contact with satanic beings (*Reincarnation and Christianity,* Bethany House, pp. 24–25, italics added).

Those are not past lives they are recalling. They're not even past spirits. They are simply demons speaking through or starting to take over the thoughts of the person who had given up control of his or her mind." (pp. 94–95)

## ▶ CHANNELING

Channeling is nothing but your basic demon possession. Of course the latest twist is that these critters are supposedly from outer space or are folks who have died. But it's all the same thing— people giving up control of their bodies for demonic spirits to come on in and take control. And

WHAT'S ALL THIS NEW AGE STUFF? **125**

what does the Bible say?

> Let no one be found among you who
> . . . practices divination or sorcery, in-
> terprets omens, engages in witchcraft,
> or casts spells, or who is a medium or
> spiritist or who consults the dead. Any-
> one who does these things is detestable
> to the Lord.
>
> Deuteronomy 18:10-12

> Do not allow a sorceress to live.
>
> Exodus 22:18

> A man or woman who is a medium or
> spiritist among you must be put to
> death. You are to stone them.
>
> Leviticus 20:27

But why? Is God afraid of a little competition?
Hardly. It's simply that demonic spirits will
always take more than they give. And if you fool
around and invite them in, there's a good chance
they won't be leaving.

## ▶ MEDITATION AND SPIRIT GUIDES

Another big fad these days is meditation—but not
the type the Bible talks about. The Bible encourages us to "meditate" on God's Word and His
greatness. New Agers tell us to let our minds go
entirely blank. BIG DIFFERENCE. Because once
we've created a vacuum inside, the New Agers
encourage us to go to the second phase: inviting
into that vacuum a "spirit guide" to "guide us
into all spiritual knowledge and maturity."

Unfortunately it's been proven over and over again that no matter how beautiful and loving the spirit guide is (it may even claim to be Jesus), in reality it's your basic, let's-possess-the-kid demon.

These are just a few of the basic New Age practices. Let's take a closer look at some of its basic beliefs.

## ▶ NEW AGE BELIEFS

As we've seen, once you strip away the Christian-sounding phrases from New Age thinking, you wind up with a religion that is definitely hazardous to your health. But that's just the beginning. Because the New Age claims are also *directly opposed* to what the Bible teaches. The charts that follow give some prime examples.

### THE KEY

*The cross.* The cross was the whole purpose of Jesus' life. The cross was main reason He came down here. Yes, He said a lot of great things and yes, He cleared up lots of questions about who God is and what He's like—but over and over Jesus kept saying He came for one thing: over and over He kept pointing to the cross.

Again and again He said He came to take our punishment, to die on the cross so we could live.

> The Son of Man [Jesus] did not come to be served, but to serve, and to give His life as a ransom for many.
>
> Matthew 20:28

# GOD

| NEW AGE THINKING | BIBLE TRUTHS |
| --- | --- |
| There are many ways that lead to God. | Jesus Christ is the *ONLY* way we can reach the Father. "I am the way and the truth and the life. No one comes to the Father except through Me" (John 14:6). |
| God is not a specific person with a personality but a "force of the universe," *a la* Star Wars. | The Bible describes a specific God with a specific personality (Jesus taught us to pray, "Our Father which art in heaven," not "Some force which is everywhere"). God is a Father who loves, who aches, who gets angry, who forgives, and most important is someone who takes a personal interest in each of us (to the point of knowing how many hairs are on our heads). |
| God is both good and evil—"the good and dark side of the force." | "Your Heavenly Father is perfect" (Matthew 5:48). In Habakkuk we read that His eyes "are too pure to look on evil" (1:13). |

# JESUS CHRIST

| NEW AGE THINKING | BIBLE TRUTHS |
|---|---|
| Jesus Christ was the way to God in His time because He had "the Christ spirit" living in Him. But other people in other ages also had this same "Christ spirit," like Hercules, Krishna, and Buddha, and they were the way to God in *their* time. | A good clue of satanic influence is when anyone tries to raise up others to share in Jesus' glory. The Bible gives no room for such blasphemy. In fact Jesus Himself clearly said, *"No one* comes to the Father except through Me" (John 14:6, italics added), "I am the first and the last" (Revelation 1:17), and "All who came before Me were thieves and robbers" (John 10:8). The Bible states clearly that Jesus Christ is the one and only way to God in the past, present, or future. |

# MAN

| NEW AGE THINKING | BIBLE TRUTHS |
|---|---|
| Man is basically good. | Right. That's why we have so many wars and killings and injustices. The Bible clearly teaches that "all have sinned and fallen short of the glory of God" (Romans 3:23), that we're born with this sin, and that the only way we can be free of it is through Jesus Christ. |
| Man is god. | This is exactly the same lie Satan used on Eve: "You will be like God" (Genesis 3:5). Hmmm. |
| Man can work his way into eternal paradise and Godlike perfection. | Once again they're saying there's no need for Christ's sacrifice on the cross, that we can do it on our own. Instead the Bible clearly states, "For it is by grace you have been saved, through faith—and this is not from yourselves, it is the gift of God—not by works, so that no one can boast" (Ephesians 2:8-9). |

There are other verses: Matthew 26:28, Luke 22:19-20, Luke 24:26, John 1:29, John 3:14-17, John 6:51, John 10:11, John 12:24-33, John 15:13, and the list goes on.

So no matter how Christian any teaching claims to be, it's a safe bet that *any belief or religion that says the Cross is not the very center of our relationship with God is NOT from God.* Can't get any simpler than that.

## ALL THIS TO SAY . . .

No one wants to start a witch-hunt here or accuse every supernatural occurrence or everything we don't understand as being from the devil (God's also been known to pull off a few supernatural events from time to time). But be careful. Just because a person is experiencing the supernatural doesn't necessarily mean he's experiencing God. There are plenty of other supernatural creatures out there that would like to get your attention—and a lot more.

If you run across one of these new teachings or have a friend that is involved in one, check it out. Find out what it REALLY says about:

● God,
● Jesus Christ,
● humankind,

and most important find out what it says about Jesus' sacrifice for us on the cross.

# HOW TO
# BE A GOOD
# CHRISTIAN IN A
# MESSED-UP WORLD

▶ Ever feel like there's a civil war going on—and it's going on right inside your head?

The world part of you is screaming, "Yeah, do it, DO IT, *DO IT!*"

And the Christian part's going, "Well, uh, I don't know, maybe, uh, maybe I shouldn't, uh. . . ."

Don't feel too bad. We all have a little of this split personality.

Even the great Apostle Paul talked about it in one of his letters:

> For the sinful nature desires what is contrary to the Spirit, and the Spirit what is contrary to the sinful nature. They are in conflict with each other.
> Galatians 5:17

## ► WHY FIGHT?

*If trying to live a decent life is such a hassle, why fight it? Why not just give in and go for the good times?*

A good question and one that makes a lot of sense except for two minor details: a miserable eternal life and a miserable current life. (Other than that, it's a great idea.)

The eternal misery isn't too hard to figure out. I mean, hell is definitely not my idea of a good time. And as far as our current lives go, remember that all those do's and don'ts from the Bible are not for God's pleasure; He gets no jollies out of being some sort of Cosmic Cop of the Universe. Those guidelines and rules are for *us;* they're to help *us* live our lives abundantly.

Now it's true, sin is fun—for a while. But, as we've said, it's just a baited hook. At first bite it may taste great. But once we've swallowed it, it starts to take control. Oh, we may not feel it at first, but eventually it will always, ALWAYS wind up taking more than it gives. In the long run sin, no matter how great it looks and tastes, will always leave us wanting. It will *always* leave us broken, empty, and suffering.

That's why we fight the war.

## ► ENEMY TACTICS

In any war it's good to know the enemy's strategy. Satan has a simple, three-point plan that goes like this:

1. CONVINCE us that the sin really isn't that

bad, that everybody else is doing it, and that the pleasures really do outweigh the cost. Oh, and let's not forget the old *"you can just nibble on the bait without having to swallow the hook"* routine. These messages are usually brought to us courtesy of our friends, the media, or peer pressure.

After we've been bombarded with these deceptive messages, the enemy goes on to the next phase.

2. CONCEIVE the sin in our thought-life. The second phase of the attack is to get us to start dwelling on the sin, allowing it to be born in our minds and take up residence there as we begin to think and imagine its pleasures over and over again.

3. CONQUER us. The last phase is to go in for the kill. All he has to do is set up the right situation—a situation where we make the simple crossover from performing the sin with our minds to performing it with our bodies—and BINGO, he's got us.

That's it; that's all he does. Yet so many of us fall for his tactics over and over and over some more.

The good news is we don't have to fall for it. The good news is that Jesus not only died on the cross for the times we lose the battle, but He also gave us the power to win!

Here's how:

## ▶ *THE BATTLE PLAN*

First of all it's important to remember that we're not in the battle alone. No matter what sin may be nagging at us, no matter how unique it may seem, others have been through it too.

> No temptation has seized you except what is common to man.
>
> 1 Corinthians 10:13

That in itself should be of some comfort—but there's more. Remember, we're not dealing with some God sitting high on some cushy throne who's never been through the battle Himself. We're dealing with Jesus—someone who, according to the Bible, has faced EVERY temptation we'll ever face.

> For we do not have a high priest [Jesus] who is unable to sympathize with our weaknesses, but we have one who has been tempted in every way, just as we are—yet was without sin.
>
> Hebrews 4:15

I don't know about you, but I feel a lot better having somebody with the Lord's experience on my side—somebody who will understand when I stumble but also somebody who has won and will show me how to do the same.

Let's look at His strategy.

### TAKE UP THE OFFENSIVE

Every coach of every team and every general of every army will tell you the same thing: the best defense is a good offense. So instead of waiting around for the enemy to fill your head with a bunch of garbage that you have to start fighting off, beat him to the punch. Start filling your head with good stuff so that there's no room for the junk.

> Whatever is true, whatever is noble, whatever is right, whatever is pure, whatever is lovely, whatever is admirable—if anything is excellent or praiseworthy—think about such things.
> Philippians 4:8

If we keep watching films and sexy soaps that trample God's values, or if we keep hanging out with friends and people that call right wrong and wrong right, Satan's already accomplished his first phase of attack—he's already infiltrated our minds.

But if we're careful to expose ourselves to quality people, quality thoughts, and quality media, there's far less space for the enemy to sneak in and set up camp.

The same is true with time. If we keep ourselves busy in quality activities, there's little time for boredom to set in and little time to contemplate crud.

Everyone says our minds are like computers. And they're right. We operate only as well as we've been programmed. And if all we do is sit back and allow the enemy to feed us garbage, then garbage is what we'll produce. But if we take up the offensive and feed our minds and our time

with excellence and quality, then that is how we'll
live.

### BELIEVE
*But what do we do when the enemy does manage
to sneak in?*

Now it starts getting interesting. Now we get
into a little hand-to-hand combat, a little trench
warfare. No one likes to fight. If you can, try to
avoid it; try to "flee from evil." But if you can't,
here's what you do. It's not always easy and it's
not always fun. But it's simple. The key word?

*BELIEVE.* Believe that, with God's help, you'll
win. Because winning is what He promises over
and over again.

> Resist the devil, and he will flee from
> you.
>
> James 4:7

> God is faithful; He will not let you be
> tempted beyond what you can bear.
> But when you are tempted, He will
> also provide a way out so that you can
> stand up under it.
>
> 1 Corinthians 10:13

Or as Paul put it:

> Sin shall not be your master.
>
> Romans 6:14

Belief. It all comes down to who we want to
put our faith in. Do we want to believe Satan,
that he'll win, or do we want to believe God, that

we'll win? It sounds simple, I know, but that's all there is to it.

> Because the One who is in you [Jesus] is greater than the one who is in the world.
>
> 1 John 4:4

But the fact that something is simple doesn't necessarily make it easy. Satan will do all he can to convince us he's more powerful than God. He will shout, he will yell, he will scream—but it's all just hot air, only distractions and attempts to get our eyes off Jesus and His promises.

It's just like Peter walking on the water in Matthew 14. Jesus told him he could and Peter did, plain and simple—but only for a while. Pretty soon the enemy started to convince Peter to take his eyes off Jesus and look instead at the howling wind and crashing waves. And it wasn't too long before old Pete started to believe that he really couldn't be doing what he was doing. As soon as he started believing Satan's distractions instead of God's promises, he sank.

The same is true with us. The only way Satan can win is to get our eyes off Jesus' promises that we'll succeed and focus them on Satan's lies that we can't.

## PRAY
This is such an obvious weapon that we often overlook it. God wants us to win these battles even more than we do. So if we ask for His help, even when we're sinking, we'll still win.

Jesus didn't leave Peter drowning in the water. Instead, as soon as Peter called out for help, Jesus reached down and brought him back up to victory. All the disciple had to do was ask.

And the same is true with us.

> All things for which you pray and ask,
> believe that you have received them,
> and they shall be granted you.
>
> Mark 11:24 (NASB)

We can accomplish anything and everything that God wants in our lives through prayer.

*Does all this mean that we'll never have to sin again?*

Yes, but don't count on it. We're humans; we make mistakes. But as we continue to grow and mature in Christ and as we continue to learn to fight the fight, our defeats and failures will become fewer and farther apart.

## ▶ SPECIFICS

So much for textbook theory. Now let's look at some practical situations. If one or more of the following are a particular battle zone in your mind, take a look at these victory suggestions.

### MATERIALISM

Everywhere from billboards to radio to magazines to TV, people are telling us to be discontent with what we have. People are telling us that if we really want to be happy, then we have to buy what they're hawking. No wonder we always want just a little more than what we have—and then a little more, and a little more. . . .

SUGGESTED SOLUTIONS: Spend more time thanking God for what you do have—even the broken and worn stuff. Often wanting *things* comes from wanting a life that's a little fuller. So find activities to fill up your life. You might even want to consider involvement in local outreaches such as those designed to help the poor. (If there's anything that will make you appreciate what you have, it's helping those who don't.)

## SEX

We've already talked quite a bit about this. But if lust is a problem in your life, consider these ideas.

SUGGESTED SOLUTIONS: Stay away from hot and steamy flicks and pics. Why give the enemy more fuel to feed the fire? If sexual daydreams are your hangup, try to keep your mind and body occupied with more wholesome stuff. And if you're dating and find yourself breaking too many rules, then it's time for a little talk with your partner. Establish some parameters; don't just keep slipping further and further without ever addressing the issue.

And as we've mentioned before, try to avoid secluded one-on-one situations and get more into group activities. Instead of the same old making out in front of the TV or steaming up the windshield, try bowling, tennis, museums, bicycling, swimming, amusement parks—that sort of stuff.

## A BIG MOUTH
Scripture has a lot to say about the sins of the mouth: gossiping, back-biting, spouting off. James probably put it best when he pointed out that although it may be one of the smallest parts of the body, the tongue often does the most damage.

SUGGESTED SOLUTIONS: Pray that God would make you more sensitive to what should and shouldn't be said. (Remember that He rates gossip right up there with murder and adultery.)

If you find your wisecracks or outbursts of temper are getting you into too much trouble, try the old count-to-10 before you respond. It's amazing how just those few seconds can give your mouth the needed self-control.

## PARENTS
Raising up parents through your teen years can be tough. But Scripture is pretty clear about honoring and respecting them.

SUGGESTED SOLUTIONS: Try to keep in mind that for the most part your parents are probably doing the best they can. But life's tough. Parents are under incredible outside pressure and don't always behave the way they want to. And to top it off there's you. . . .

The little kid that worshiped the ground they walked on is now embarrassed to be seen in the same car with them. And if that's not tough enough to swallow, their precious, cuddly, little bundle of joy is suddenly demanding to be treated like an adult.

Change and transition are tough. As a teen you're going through more than most parents can keep up with. In a very real way the person you were yesterday is not entirely the person you are today . . . or will be tomorrow. And as tough as that may be for you, I guarantee that these transitions are even tougher on your parents.

So if you can, give them some slack; try to understand their predicament. And, above all, ask God for help. Remember, although they may be blowing it, the bottom line is that most parents love their children deeply. And, believe it or not, if it came down to it, they'd probably lay down their very lives for yours.

## PEER PRESSURE
Many sociologists agree that, next to the family, no single force affects a teen's behavior more than peer pressure. Why? And how can we use it to our advantage?

SUGGESTED SOLUTIONS: Almost all people are susceptible to peer pressure. But those who have the most problems with it are those who simply don't know how important they are. They don't understand how deeply God loves and values them. So they count their worth by what others think. They live in fear of how others will accept them. They want to be liked and will go along with the crowd (even when the crowd is wrong) so they'll feel loved.

Yet, if they really took the time with God (in prayer and in His Word), they'd eventually understand how deep and far-reaching His love is for them. And, suddenly, what others think really wouldn't make that much difference. In many respects this is exactly what the Bible means when it says that God's "perfect love drives out fear" (1 John 4:18).

### ALL THIS TO SAY . . .

These are just five examples of today's typical temptations and some suggestions on how to beat them. But the bottom line is this:

Temptations will come; the battles will rage. But we don't have to live in defeat. The Bible promises that we're not in this alone; we have a great Champion on our side. If we call on that Champion's power, we can always beat the enemy. All we have to do is believe; all we have to do is "fight the good fight of faith" (1 Timothy 6:12). Because . . .

> In all these things we are *more than conquerors* through Him who loved us.
>
> Romans 8:37 (italics added)

# MORE GREAT SONPOWER BOOKS BY BILL MYERS

*Hot Topics, Tough Questions*
In the original of the "Hot Topics" duo you'll discover the Bible's answers to your hardest questions. Find out what God says about sex and dating, the media, the occult, and other important topics. Catalog no. 6-2517

*Faith Workout*
Exercise your faith and watch it grow stronger with this study of the Book of James. Find out how to deal with such areas as temptation, the tongue, and money. Catalog no. 6-2265

*Jesus: An Eyewitness Account*
Take a life-changing look at Jesus through the Gospel of John. Get the inside story on what He did *then* and what difference it makes *now*. Catalog no. 6-1606

Leader's Guides with Multiuse Transparency Masters and Rip-Offs are available.

Buy these titles at your local Christian bookstore or order from SP Publications, Inc., 1825 College Ave., Wheaton, IL 60187.